Every pastor needs a strong small group ministry, and every pastor needs someone who understands Sunday School principles and knows how to work with others to implement them. God blessed this pastor and First Baptist Woodstock with such a man in Allan Taylor. In his book *Sunday School in HD* you will discover how to use your Sunday School to develop leaders and grow your church. If you want to see the details of that plan as clear as the images on your high definition television, then read on! If you want to grow your church through an HD Sunday School, just implement the principles Allan shares. Read and reread, then pass this book on to everyone in your Sunday School.

Dr. Johnny Hunt
Southern Baptist Convention President
Pastor, First Baptist Church
Woodstock, Georgia

As an active member of First Baptist Woodstock, I have come to appreciate Allan Taylor's dedication to fulfilling the Great Commission through the Sunday School strategy. Having served under Allan's leadership as a Sunday School teacher, I have come to appreciate the simplicity and effectiveness of his ministry plan. The principles in *Sunday School in HD* will work for churches of any size or age, and Allan's skill in sharing those principles will make it simple for you to implement. Allan Taylor and *Sunday School in HD* get my vote!

Sonny Perdue
Governor, State of Georgia

If you want to pump new life into your church, then *Sunday School in HD* is for you. No one knows the work of Sunday School better than Allan Taylor. He gives a clear job description for involving Christians in small groups in the local church.

Dr. Ted Traylor
Pastor, Olive Baptist Church
Pensacola, Florida

Using his unique, conversational style, Allan has written a must-have book for every pastor and church leader. If you think Sunday School is outdated, you'd better think again! This book is packed with tons of practical, usable insights you can use to make Sunday School the growth engine of your church.

Donnie Smith
Senior Group VP, Poultry and Prepared Foods
Tyson Foods Inc.
Bible Study Teacher
First Baptist Church of Springdale
Springdale, Arkansas

Allan has provided a clear template for how to build a Sunday School that soars! No matter the size and no matter the place, if you are looking for real answers, you have definitely picked up the right book. I'm buying one for every staff member at Prestonwood. I only wish it would have been available earlier.

Jeff Young
Minister of Spiritual Development
Prestonwood Baptist Church
Dallas, Texas

After reading Allan Taylor's *Sunday School in HD*, I am more convinced than ever that he is this generation's Arthur Flake. In a very simple, easy to read fashion, he makes clear that Sunday School is the church organized to fulfill her mission. He also validates that Sunday School is still the *single most effective* Bible teaching, reaching, and ministering arm of church. Whether you have thought about abandoning Sunday School or still believe in its effectiveness, this book is an absolute must read!

Mark Rush
Executive Pastor
Immanuel Baptist Church
Highland, California

SUNDAY SCHOOL IN HD

SUNDAY SCHOOL IN HD

Sharpening the Focus on What Makes Your Church Healthy

ALLAN TAYLOR

NASHVILLE, TENNESSEE

Printed in the United States of America

ISBN: 978-0-8054-4973-0

Published by B&H Publishing Group
Nashville, Tennessee

Dewey Decimal Classification: 268
Subject Heading: SUNDAY SCHOOLS—GROWTH

1 2 3 4 5 6 7 8 • 13 12 11 10 09

Contents

Acknowledgments

This book is dedicated to the wonderful Sunday School teachers and leaders of First Baptist Church, Woodstock, Georgia. Their love for Christ, His Word, and His bride is unparalleled. It has been my absolute joy to serve with this greatest assembled group of Sunday School workers anywhere!

Foreword

Allan Taylor. Sunday School.

One is a person's name. The other is an organizational name. But, for many of us, the names are synonyms. Allan Taylor has truly become "Mr. Sunday School" for the twenty-first century. His contributions to this vital ministry, even at this relatively young part of his life, are legendary.

I remember meeting Allan for the first time. There were many things about him that impressed me. He was enthusiastic about life and ministry. He was passionate about his calling. He was devoted and loyal to his senior pastor, Dr. Johnny Hunt. He loved his church, First Baptist Church of Woodstock, Georgia. He was a devoted family man.

But what I remember most about Allan was his desire to equip others for the work of ministry. That reality was evident in his hours of labor for conferences and mentoring ministers in other churches. That reality was further evident in his work to write material for others to use in their ministry. The predecessor volume to this book, *Six Core Values of Sunday School*, is a great example of his equipping ministry.

Yet, when the final curtain is drawn, I believe that the most lasting impact of Allan Taylor's ministry will be his leadership and passion for Sunday School. You see, Allan is a contrarian. He understands that Sunday School is not the newest or the most innovative ministry of this century. He understands that many church leaders do not see great value in this multi-century ministry. He understands all of those realities. But he refuses to believe that Sunday School is a dinosaur headed for extinction. He is truly a contrarian.

Why?

Perhaps it is because he continues to see Sunday School as a tremendous outreach and evangelistic arm of the church. Perhaps it is because he understands that Sunday School is a vital place for the local church to express her core values. Or perhaps it is because he sees Sunday School as the place where Christians can easily become involved in ministry. Perhaps it is because he sees the Bible teaching ministry of Sunday School as one of the most successful venues for equipping others for ministry. Or perhaps it is because he has seen for years how Sunday School develops others for leadership.

Allan Taylor is a contrarian—a contrarian who has it right.

Sunday School in HD is a book that needs to be in the hands of millions of church staff and laity. It is a book, if taken to heart, that can radically change a church toward health and biblical growth. It is a book that will bless you, for it is certainly a book that blessed me.

One caution is needed before you proceed. This book will not offer you a quick-fix solution for greater health in your church. Indeed, if you approach this book as yet another add-on methodology, put it down right now.

Building a healthy Sunday School is hard work. Allan does not hide that issue. But that hard work can lead a church to make disciples and to move toward true biblical health. The effort is worth it.

I am blessed to know Allan Taylor.

I am blessed by having read *Sunday School in HD.*

And I am blessed to know that many readers of this book will take its truths and applications seriously, and thus Christ's churches will be healthier.

To God be the glory.

Thom S. Rainer
President and CEO
LifeWay Christian Resources

Introduction

On the morning of July 4, 1952, thirty-four-year-old Florence Chadwick attempted to swim the twenty-one-mile strait between Catalina Island and the coast of California. Having already conquered the English Channel in both directions, she was a veteran to long-distance swimming, but on this day the water was cold and the fog so thick she could scarcely see the boats that accompanied her.

After fifteen grueling hours she quit despite encouragement from those in the boat. She later realized that she was a mere half-mile from her destination. When questioned later by a reporter about her decision to stop, she said, "I'm not excusing myself, but if I could have seen the shore, I might have made it." Florence failed to reach her goal because she could not see. The fog prevented her from seeing her destination and knowing how close she was to it.

A few months after Florence Chadwick failed in her attempt to swim the twenty-one-mile strait off the coast of California, she made a second attempt. The second attempt, like the first, was in the midst of a thick fog. This time, however, she was successful. When asked why she made it the second time with a similar thick fog, she reportedly replied, "This time the shore was in my heart!"

Sunday School seems to have a thick fog surrounding it to the point that some have a hard time seeing and understanding it clearly. Like Florence Chadwick we have lost sight of our destination. But, I believe it is vital we continue to focus on this proven tool for church growth and health.

Do you want your Sunday School to grow? Of course everyone answers a resounding "Yes!" Then why are Sunday Schools not growing? In my own Southern Baptist Convention the average worship attendance is 137, and the average Sunday School attendance is ninety-three. These numbers reflect neither good nor bad attendance; they just reflect reality. The number that jumps off the page to me is the decline in Sunday School enrollment. Last year Sunday School enrollment in the convention dropped 55,142; that's fifty-five megachurches!

The original question is an easy one to answer, and most everyone would answer yes. But the important question is, are you willing to pay the price for growth? When I was coaching high school football, we would get our team together after the Christmas break to start the dreaded winter workouts. We would pose the question, "How many of you want to win the championship next year?" Of course that elicited a unanimous vote. Then we would ask the question, "How many of you are willing to pay the price to win the championship next year?" That, my friend, was the real question. Certainly everyone wants to win the championship, but will everyone show up three mornings a week at 6:30 a.m. to work out?

What is causing us to have decreasing Sunday Schools rather than increasing Sunday Schools? It is not a lack of desire to have a growing Sunday School. It is our unwillingness to pay the price! Growth requires two things. First, it requires change. The well-worn definition of *insanity* applies here: to continue to do what you have always done and expect different results. If we always do what we have always done, we will always get what we have always gotten! Change is imperative for growth whether it is on a personal or an organizational level. The second thing growth requires is commitment. Commitment is what takes good ideas and turns them into reality. Commitment is not realized until personal convenience is jeopardized.

I still believe that Sunday School works! Many have pronounced her dead on arrival saying she is a worn-out method of a foregone era. Many naysayers proclaim Sunday School as no longer effective in a modern day. It is outdated and no longer has an appeal they say. Many reject it simply because it is "traditional." Take caution! We need to be careful in discarding something simply because it is traditional. If we want to eliminate tradition in the church, then we will have to purge our churches of preaching, prayer, fellowship, Bible study, offerings, soul winning, discipleship, and worship. All are traditional and have been practiced by the church since Pentecost!

Sunday School is only as effective as those leading it and working it. When we do work the Sunday School fields, a harvest can be reaped. It is with this in mind that I present this book. I believe Sunday Schools should explode with growth as we practice the three tasks of Sunday School—reach people, teach people, and minister to people.

Sunday School is overlooked and underworked. Today's fog around Sunday School is causing many not to *see* it; hence, it is overlooked, and because it is overlooked, it is naturally underworked. Enter *Sunday School in HD*. If we will *see* Sunday School for what it is and what it can do, we will all champion her cause! However, we can only *see* it as we can define it. A high-definition Sunday School needs clarity in five areas.

- The Role of Sunday School in HD
- The Purpose of Sunday School in HD
- The Growth of Sunday School in HD
- The Leadership of Sunday School in HD
- The Passion of Sunday School in HD

It is my prayer that what is addressed in this book will move your Sunday School from just surviving to thriving. I suggest that you read my original book on Sunday School, *The Six Core Values of Sunday School*. It will serve as a companion to this book, and the two will complement each other. Blessings!

Allan Taylor
Minister of Education
First Baptist Church
Woodstock, Georgia

THE ROLE OF SUNDAY SCHOOL IN HD

---

role: a part played; a position or function (*Webster's II New College Dictionary*)

CHAPTER 1

The Vital Contribution of Sunday School

As a young boy I did not have high-definition television. In fact, we did not have color television. Our family TV was black-and-white. Now go ahead and reach for your handkerchief because we only had three channels from which to select—NBC, CBS, and, if the aluminum foil on the rabbit ears was just right, ABC. Boy, have things ever changed. Television has been around for decades, and it has made drastic improvements.

Like television, Sunday School has been around for decades. Most churches still have a functioning Sunday School. However, many questions have been raised as to the validity of Sunday School in an ever-changing world. What is the benefit of a Sunday School ministry in a local church? What role does Sunday School play in the context of the church's ministry? Does Sunday School fulfill a vital function in helping the church reach her mission? Are we just having Sunday School because we have always had Sunday School? Is it a worn-out method of yesteryear? Does Sunday School still have relevancy in the twenty-first century? These questions beg to see the context of Sunday School in the contemporary church. They seek to know if Sunday School has a vital contribution to make in the life and ministry of a local church. I want to give you six reasons why

Sunday School is still a relevant, vital, and necessary ingredient in producing growing disciples and healthy churches.

Sunday School Is Relevant

1. Sunday School gives the church's DNA a natural, functional, practical expression.

I serve the First Baptist Church of Woodstock, Georgia. Under the leadership of our pastor, Dr. Johnny Hunt, we have adopted a fourfold mission for our church that we refer to as our church's DNA. Our mission is to:

- Worship God
- Love Others
- Serve God
- Invite Others

We want every member to be a disciple who loves God with his whole being in accordance with the first and greatest commandment. We want every member to love others, the second great commandment. We want every member to find a place of service and activate their spiritual gifts. We also want every believer to invite others to know Christ, to witness to them, and to invite them to church where they will hear the gospel. These four things are the ingredients of a disciple of Jesus Christ. These four things are the mission of First Baptist Woodstock. They are also the four things we want every one of our members to embrace because they are the church. We need a way to express our DNA, and Sunday School makes that possible in three ways.

Sunday School gives a *natural* expression to the church's DNA. It is natural for a believer to want to be discipled, build community with others, minister to people's needs, and be on mission with others in the body of Christ. As believers, we naturally desire a supernatural lifestyle because of the One who loves us and lives within us.

> As His *divine power* has given to us all things that pertain to life and godliness, through the knowledge of Him who called us by glory and virtue, by which have been given to us exceedingly great and precious promises, that through these you may be partakers of the *divine nature*, having escaped the corruption that is in the world through lust. (2 Pet. 1:3–4, *emphasis mine*)

Through His divine power God has given us everything we need to live supernaturally. He has even invested His divine nature in us through the person of the Holy Spirit. We need to find a natural way to express that which is naturally in us, and Sunday School fills this need. Sunday School provides a natural mechanism for every believer to express naturally what is supernaturally in them. We have the purpose in our heads and hearts; Sunday School moves it to our hands and feet! Sunday School affords every member a natural way to express the church's mission.

Sunday School gives a *functional* expression to the church's DNA. The book of Acts gives us the fivefold purpose of the church: worship, evangelism, discipleship, ministry, and fellowship. All of these, with the exception of worship, function better through Sunday School than through the corporate worship service. We have a clear mental picture of these five functions; however, they practically take place through the ministry of small groups.

Sunday School gives a *practical* expression to the church's DNA. Most of us know *what* to do; it is finding the *how* that is challenging. Sunday School is the *how* behind the *what*. Our pastors stand in our pulpits and proclaim the Word of God. Their messages tell us what to be and what to do. However, we leave the worship service with no tangible, practical way to express what we just heard. I am afraid that we teach a theology that never gets out of the intellectual and into the practical. Certainly we need to be good thinkers and to be intellectually astute so we can engage lost people who have bought into the lies and deceitfulness of the devil. At the same time, unbelievers must see a practical expression of our sound theology as it is lived out in the context of a real world that is reeling in pain and despair. At some point our theological and practical hands must shake!

Sunday School becomes a vital tool for the church to express her core values. I have found that without a tool, our values often go unexpressed. When I was a boy, my Granny used to put my three brothers and me to work in the garden. With school out for the summer, she had to find productive things for us to do to keep us out of trouble. About once a week she would take me to the garden to weed. She would hand me the hoe and instruct me to rid the garden of the weeds. Granny gave me a task: weed the garden. She also gave me a tool to accomplish the task: a hoe. In the church we are guilty of giving people the task without the tool to accomplish that task. Sunday School puts a hoe in all believers' hands for their work in the church garden.

Sunday School becomes a vital tool for the church to express her core values.

Can a church grow if she does not have a natural, functional, and practical way to express her purpose? It is very doubtful. Sunday School develops missional Christians as each class engages its members in the church's mission. Sunday School drives the mission down and places it on a personal basis. Many churches fail to see their mission accomplished because the mission is imprisoned behind the bars of the theological and philosophical cells. Sunday School releases the mission into the real world of practical living.

2. Mission is best accomplished in the context of small groups.

Any mission is best tackled in a setting of small groups of people. This gives everyone an opportunity for *input*. Dr. Johnny Hunt has taught me that people pay for what they own. I have found that to be true in my life. I pay for my house, my car, and my belongings. Why? They are mine! I do not make your house or car payments because I do not own them, and I have no part of them. When people are given the privilege to speak into the process, they begin to take ownership of it. If everything is dictated to people, then they will not own that mission. As we meet in small groups, people have the opportunity to speak to the mission that is being pursued by that small group. If a large meeting is the only gathering of God's people, then you run the risk of creating a dictator. Sunday School classes provide a forum for people to speak into the mission, to invest in the mission, and to own the mission.

Small groups not only give people an opportunity for input; they also give everyone an opportunity for *involvement*. A church cannot survive without the involvement of others. I have often said that the secret to success is the involvement of people! Sunday School allows people to get involved in ministry. Sunday School empowers people and puts them to work. Sunday School gives practical application of the words of Jesus, "Engage . . . until I come back" (Luke 19:13 HCSB). Let me give you three biblical examples of the principle that "mission is best accomplished in the context of small groups."

Sunday School empowers people and puts them to work.

> And so it was, on the next day, that Moses sat to judge the people; and the people stood before Moses from morning until evening. So when Moses' father-in-law saw all that he did for the people, he said, "What is this thing that you are doing for the people? Why do you alone sit, and all the people stand before you from morning until evening?" And Moses said to his father-in-law, "Because the people come to me to inquire of God. When they have a difficulty, they come to me, and I judge between one and another; and I make known the statutes of God and His laws." So Moses' father-in-law said to him, "The thing that you do is not good. Both you

> and these people who are with you will surely wear yourselves out. For this thing is too much for you; you are not able to perform it by yourself. Listen now to my voice; I will give you counsel, and God will be with you: Stand before God for the people, so that you may bring the difficulties to God. And you shall teach them the statutes and the laws, and show them the way in which they must walk and the work they must do. Moreover you shall select from all the people able men, such as fear God, men of truth, hating covetousness; and place such over them to be rulers of thousands, rulers of hundreds, rulers of fifties, and rulers of tens. And let them judge the people at all times. Then it will be that every great matter they shall bring to you, but every small matter they themselves shall judge. So it will be easier for you, for they will bear the burden with you. If you do this thing, and God so commands you, then you will be able to endure, and all this people will also go to their place in peace." So Moses heeded the voice of his father-in-law and did all that he had said. And Moses chose able men out of all Israel, and made them heads over the people: rulers of thousands, rulers of hundreds, rulers of fifties, and rulers of tens. So they judged the people at all times; the hard cases they brought to Moses, but they judged every small case themselves. (Exod. 18:13–26)

In this passage we see the mission is to judge the people. Moses, the great leader of God, sat all day judging the grievances of the people. Moses was getting weary and so were the people. Jethro, Moses' father-in-law, advised him to get some help, divide the people into smaller groups, and appoint capable men over jurisdictions. They were to be "rulers of thousands, rulers of hundreds, rulers of fifties, and rulers of tens."

Moses reminds me of some pastors today. They are working hard but not working smart. I have had the blessing of doing conferences in many countries. Over and over again, I see two people in churches doing the entire ministry—the pastor and the worship leader. They are godly men, working hard, loving their people, trying to meet all their needs, erecting buildings, and trying to win their communities to faith in Christ. They are worn out and need some help. Like Moses, they need to be asked, "Why do you sit alone?" (Exod. 18:14). They need a Jethro to step into their life with exhortation, "The thing that you do is not good. Both you and these people who are with you will surely wear yourselves out. For this thing is too much for you; you are not able to perform it by yourself" (Exod. 18:17–18).

They need to heed the advice of Jethro and find capable people and release ministry to them. I submit to you that Sunday School is that ministry! I have seen pastors all over the world light up when they have caught the vision of getting others involved in vital ministry. Yet I constantly see American churches that are more exposed to the concept of ministry through Sunday School not get it. In some cases they are *having* Sunday School but they are not *using* Sunday School.

In some cases they are *having* Sunday School but they are not *using* Sunday School.

> *When the mission was to judge the people, Moses learned that "mission is best accomplished in the context of a small group."*

Ezra and Nehemiah observed this principle being practiced in their day.

> Now all the people gathered together as one man in the open square that was in front of the Water Gate; and they told Ezra the scribe to bring the Book of the Law of Moses, which the Lord had commanded

> Israel. So Ezra the priest brought the Law before the assembly of men and women and all who could hear with understanding on the first day of the seventh month. Then he read from it in the open square that was in front of the Water Gate from morning until midday, before the men and women and those who could understand; and the ears of all the people were attentive to the Book of the Law. So Ezra the scribe stood on a platform of wood which they had made for the purpose; and beside him, at his right hand, stood Mattithiah, Shema, Anaiah, Urijah, Hilkiah, and Maaseiah; and at his left hand Pedaiah, Mishael, Malchijah, Hashum, Hashbadana, Zechariah, and Meshullam. And Ezra opened the book in the sight of all the people, for he was standing above all the people; and when he opened it, all the people stood up. And Ezra blessed the Lord, the great God. Then all the people answered, "Amen, Amen!" while lifting up their hands. And they bowed their heads and worshiped the Lord with their faces to the ground. Also Jeshua, Bani, Sherebiah, Jamin, Akkub, Shabbethai, Hodijah, Maaseiah, Kelita, Azariah, Jozabad, Hanan, Pelaiah, and the Levites, helped the people to understand the Law: and the people stood in their place. So they read distinctly from the book, in the Law of God; and they gave the sense, and helped them to understand the reading. (Neh. 8:1–8)

In 586 BC the Babylonians had destroyed the magnificent temple that King Solomon had built. Some poor Jews were allowed to remain in the land of Israel, but most were carried away to Babylonian captivity. A remnant had returned, but they lived under much scrutiny and persecution. Under the prophetic ministry of Haggai and Zechariah and the leadership of Zerubbabel, the people rebuilt the temple.

Some seventy-five years later under Nehemiah's godly leadership, the people rebuilt the walls of the city. Then Ezra, the scribe of God, stood at the Water Gate and read the Torah to God's chosen people from morning to noon. For many, it was the first time they had heard God's Word. Many did not understand it and needed further instruction. The Scripture says that "Jeshua, Bani, Sherebiah, Jamin, Akkub, Shabbethai, Hodijah, Maaseiah, Kelita, Azariah, Jozabad, Hanan, Pelaiah, and the Levites, helped the people to understand the Law." The Bible does not give the exact details of how this took place, but it does give us the names of thirteen teachers who helped people understand the meaning of the Scripture read by Ezra. This passage also informs us that the Levites also helped to teach the people the meaning of what they had heard. How many Levites were there? The Scripture does not indicate. It would seem that there would have been many. Therefore, these many teachers must have huddled in smaller groups with people to explain the teaching of the Scripture. I have written in the margin of my Bible beside this Scripture "The first organized Sunday School."

> *You see, when the mission was to help the people understand the Word of God, Ezra and Nehemiah learned that "mission is best accomplished in the context of a small group."*

In this passage we actually have a biblical account of small group Bible study for the purpose of helping people understand and live the truths of Scripture, and we have not been able to improve on it since!

The last biblical example I offer for your consideration comes from Jesus feeding the five thousand men with the little boy's lunch of five loaves and two fish.

> And the apostles, when they had returned, told Him all that they had done. Then He took them and went aside privately into a deserted place belonging to the city called Bethsaida. But when the multitudes

> know it, they followed Him; and He received them and spoke to them about the kingdom of God, and healed those who had need of healing. When the day began to wear away, the twelve came and said to Him, "Send the multitude away, that they may go into the surrounding towns and country, and lodge and get provisions; for we are in a deserted place here." But He said to them, "You give them something to eat." And they said, "We have no more than five loaves and two fish, unless we go and buy food for all these people." For there were about five thousand men. Then He said to His disciples, "Make them sit down in groups of fifty." And they did so, and made them all sit down. Then He took the five loaves and the two fish, and looking up to heaven, He blessed and broke them, and gave them to the disciples to set before the multitude. So they all ate and were filled, and twelve baskets of the leftover fragments were taken up by them. (Luke 9:10–17)

The people had been with Jesus all day as He was teaching and healing. Apparently they had missed some meals to be with Jesus (There is a message in that!). As the day began to be late, Jesus knew they needed to eat and sent His disciples into the crowd to see if they could find some food. They came back with five loaves of bread and two fish. Jesus took the food and then gave a directive to His disciples to "make them sit down in groups of fifty." Jesus knew that He could best accomplish the task of feeding the people if they were in smaller groups of fifty.

> *When the mission was to feed the people, Jesus knew that "mission is best accomplished in the context of a small group."*

Sunday School allows a church to break its mission down in bite-size, chewable, digestible pieces. It makes the mission something to get your arms around. It makes the mission doable. Sunday School creates many "ministry teams" throughout the whole church so that everyone can connect to the intended purpose of the church. It is obvious that even the early church met in a large group setting and in small group settings.

Sunday School allows a church to break its mission down in bite-size, chewable, digestible pieces.

> And daily in the *temple* (large group setting), and in every *house* (small group setting), they did not cease teaching and preaching Jesus as the Christ." (Acts 5:42, *emphasis mine*)
>
> Remember that mission is *best accomplished in the context of a small group!*

3. Sunday School equips the saints to do the work of the ministry.

Ephesians 4:11–12 is God's formula for church growth.

> And He Himself gave some to be apostles, some prophets, some evangelists, and some pastors and teachers, for equipping of the saints for the work of ministry, for the edifying of the body of Christ.

We have not found a better way to "equip the saints" than Sunday School. We have not found a better way to do "the work of the ministry" than Sunday School. We have not found a better way to "edify the body of Christ" than Sunday School! Sunday School disciples people in the Word of God. Sunday School puts people to work doing the ministry and exercising their spiritual gifts. Therefore, Sunday School is in the business of edifying the people of God like nothing else. This ought to cause many to rise up and champion her cause!

I have had the opportunity to address classes at some of our seminaries. It is such a thrill to speak to our upcoming church leaders. When addressing those preparing to be pastors, I would start out by asking, "When you finish your theological education and a church calls you to be their pastor, are you going to preach the Great Commission?" I then quoted Matthew 28:19–20. Those young seminarians would respond with a hearty "amen." I then asked, "When you finish your theological education and a church calls you to be their pastor, are you going to preach Ephesians 4:11–12?" Again, I quoted this passage of Scripture and the "amen" was even louder. I then asked one last question, "When you finish your theological training and a church calls you to be their pastor, how are you practically and tangibly going to flesh out the Great Commission and Ephesians 4:11–12?" Silence! You could have heard a pin drop; there was no comment, no response, and no amen. I let the silence linger because it was preaching a loud message: it is one thing to preach it; it is another thing to do it! Now I believe in the power of preaching because I believe in the power of the Word, but at some point spiritual leaders must help people get practical with the Word of God. Nehemiah exhorted the people to rebuild the walls of Jerusalem, but there came a time when he started mixing mortar and laying bricks!

We have not found a better way to "equip the saints" than Sunday School.

We have not found a better way to help people become doers of the Word than through Sunday School! I challenge anyone to tell me what has done a better job of fleshing out Ephesians 4:11–12 than Sunday School. Let me repeat myself, this ought to cause many to rise up and champion her cause!

Sunday School has had to find ways to equip people to do ministry because . . .

- Sunday School cannot survive unless she does. It takes multitudes of people to supply workers needed in all age divisions.
- Sunday School is the largest organization in the church (in most cases). Therefore, Sunday School must shoulder the responsibility of equipping the people of the church. If left to a smaller ministry, the church would die for a lack of equipped people.
- Sunday School gives away hands-on ministry to people who must be trained in order to be effective.
- Sunday School empowers people with the ministry. Sunday School does not confine the people of God, she turns them loose to serve God with great zeal and passion.

4. Sunday School develops leadership for the church.

As we have just seen, Sunday School develops many for the work of Sunday School, but she also equips people for the work of other ministries in the church. If you were to eliminate Sunday School, you would see a gradual decline in workers being produced in other ministries as well. Sunday School is the foundational ministry from which other ministries are able to sprout.

How effective would other ministries in the church be if there were no Sunday School? Can you imagine ministries with leaders that had never been nurtured and discipled in a Sunday School class? For example, how effective would Awana leaders, discipleship teachers, altar counselors, evangelism trainers, counselors leading devotions at children's/youth camp, DiscipleNow Weekend, and others, be if they were not nurtured by a Sunday School class? At the least we would have to say that they probably would not be as equipped as they could be.

5. Sunday School gives intentionality to our good intentions.

Good intentions alone are no better than no intentions unless we get intentional about our good intentions! Most of us do not suffer from a lack of knowledge, but from a lack of will. Churches are full of good intentions. Churches have good intentions to win the lost, assimilate new people, disciple the saved, minister to people's needs, be on mission to reach the world, involve people in vital ministries, build relationships with others, and so on. With all these good intentions, why are we not growing and thriving? Why are most churches in decline or plateaued? There is a lack of intentionality! Friend, if good intentions would have gotten the job done, we would have won the world to Christ years ago.

Christian people often go to bed with the good intention of rising the next morning and spending time reading their Bible and praying. Yet many do not. Why? There is a lack of intentionality. They do not get to bed in time to get a decent night's rest, or they do not set the alarm early enough to have time for their morning devotions. They have good intentions; they just do not execute those intentions. Churches are like the people in them; they are full of good intentions but often devoid of ways to execute them.

As previously stated, Sunday School gives everyone the opportunity to get involved in the church's mission. Intentionality requires involvement! No involvement, no intentionality! If a church has no small group ministry, she greatly reduces the possibility for people to be involved. If you have no intentional way to get people involved, then you

- waste God's giftedness in them
- have very little ministry taking place
- raise up lazy Christians
- confine the church's potential
- position the church for an implosion

I heard a story that illustrates this point. A young preacher had graduated from seminary and was called to pastor his first church in a rural community. He had just moved to his new church when the local funeral home director called and asked him to do the graveside service for a ninety-three-year-old man. Obviously the new pastor wanted to get involved with the community and minister to the people there, so he accepted the offer. The elderly man had outlived his friends and had just a few family members so the decision was made to have only a graveside service at a small country cemetery. The funeral home director explained directions to the cemetery and gave the new pastor the time and date. At the appointed time the pastor drove to the cemetery but lost his way. Finally, after several wrong turns he showed up thirty minutes late. The hearse was gone and no people were present. The pastor just assumed the few people that would have attended decided to leave. Since he had promised he would do the graveside service, he was bound to keep his word, so he could at least report this to the funeral home director and maintain his integrity as the new pastor in town. So he took his Bible, got out of his car, and walked to the grave. It was then he noticed the workers sitting under a shade tree eating their lunch. Apparently, they were waiting on him to do the service so they could cover the grave. The pastor went to the grave and found the vault already in place. He opened his Bible and read Psalm 23, made a few comments, and offered a prayer. As he returned to his car, he overheard one of the workers say to the other, "Do you think we ought to tell him that's a septic tank?" The pastor had good intentions, but his good intentions were not enough. We must put some intentionality to our good intentions, or else we will end up with an unhealthy church on our hands.

Intentionality requires involvement! No involvement, no intentionality!

If you have no way to exercise your good intentions, then you will end up like the following story.

Everybody, Somebody, Anybody, and Nobody

> There were four church members named *Everybody*, *Somebody*, *Anybody*, and *Nobody*. There was an important job to be done, and *Everybody* was sure that *Somebody* would do it. *Anybody* could have done it, but *Nobody* did it. *Somebody* got angry about that because it was *Everybody's* job. *Everybody* thought *Anybody* could do it, but *Nobody* realized that *Everybody* wouldn't do it. It ended up that *Everybody* blamed *Somebody* when *Nobody* did what *Anybody* could have done. (Author Unknown)

6. Sunday School keeps the church small.

Everyone wants to attend a growing church that is reaching many people yet remains small. Sunday School helps keep the church small. As the population increases and more and more people move to metropolitan areas, we have seen the emergence of many megachurches. Whether your church is a megachurch or not, she should be a growing church. I believe it is God's will that everyone repent and come to faith in Christ.

> The Lord is not slack concerning His promise, as some count slackness, but is longsuffering toward us, not willing that any should perish but that all should come to repentance. (2 Pet. 3:9)

I believe it is God's will for churches to grow because it is God's will for everyone to be saved; however, a growing church faces the serious challenge of becoming bigger, and many people do not like to attend big churches. We do not have the option of not reaching more people, but we do have the challenge of accommodating people into a larger congregation. Since large congregations can be intimidating to many, how do we help people get assimilated into our growing churches? Sunday School!

Sunday School keeps the church small because Sunday School makes the church personal and relational. This places people in an environment where they are comfortable. It positions people in surroundings that are conducive to their emotional and social well-being. God designed us for relationships, and relationships are best formed in small group settings. We recognize the spiritual experience that church attendance provides, but it also offers social experiences, and we need both.

Churches work hard at reaching new people. Much time, effort, and money are expended to reach others for Christ and church membership. Yet sometimes little energy is given to assimilate those we reach. Companies have a difficult time staying in business if they cannot keep their customers. They do much in the way of marketing to acquire new customers, but they also do much in maintaining their current clients. Business is much better when you have repeat customers instead of one-time customers. So it is with the church. How do we keep the new people we reach? How do we assimilate new members? We do this through relationships! Where are relationships formed? They are formed in small group settings. Sunday School is the church's Velcro.

Sunday School puts a face to the church and presents the characteristics of smaller churches such as a hand of fellowship, a prayer of support, a hug in difficult times. Therefore, the larger a church grows, the more vital Sunday School becomes! When we stop to analyze the role that Sunday School fills in the context of a local church, it is mind-boggling. Every church needs a small group ministry. If a church has no small group ministry or has a dysfunctional small group ministry, then it leaves a huge hole in the church. I submit to you that Sunday School is the best small group ministry known to the modern-day church. The contribution of Sunday School to the church ministry cannot be overstated.

THE PURPOSE OF SUNDAY SCHOOL IN HD

---

purpose: the object toward which one strives or for which something exists (*Webster's II New College Dictionary*)

CHAPTER 2

An Imploded Sunday School

As I was sitting at home watching the news one evening, a clip from a personal camera was shown of a floor collapsing during a wedding reception. People were having a good time dancing, talking, laughing, and eating when suddenly the floor gave way and caved in. Many were injured and one killed. It was later determined that the building was poorly designed and the structure was inadequate for the amount of people attending the wedding reception.

Like the building hosting the wedding reception, Sunday School must have the proper philosophical structure in place to direct her ministry. One can only stack so many objectives onto an organization. Sunday School is ultimately not about buildings, organizational charts, record keeping, literature, and job descriptions. These are all important and certainly have their place. Sunday School is ultimately about people, and people need a philosophical structure within which to fit, move, and operate. Therefore, we must construct our "Sunday School house" in a way that moves us toward accomplishing our tasks. Without the needed undergirding we make our "Sunday School house" vulnerable to an implosion. Anytime a building implodes it injures and even kills innocent people. If church leaders neglect to direct Sunday School properly, we inevitably hurt people. We waste the very thing that we are to enhance. If this takes place, an imploded Sunday School will become a certain calamity, and mayhem will result. When this tragedy strikes, it leaves people spiritually crippled and maimed.

A well-constructed "Sunday School house" promotes a means for getting the work done and fulfilling the reason for her existence. The building itself will not secure success, but it will position people in an environment conducive for fruitful ministry. Sunday School seeks to develop and lead people to become Great Commission Christians that are involved in reaching people, teaching people, and ministering to people.

We must occasionally stop and ask ourselves if we are building an imploded house or an impregnable house. Building an impregnable Sunday School starts with the foundation. Any builder knows that the most important part of a building is its foundation. A weak foundation produces a building that is headed for an implosion. This is why building codes and building inspectors exist. They ensure that certain standards are met, especially with the foundations. They are present when foundations are laid and take samples of the concrete and send it off to laboratories to be tested for strength and endurance to prevent any possible implosion. When you have a poor foundation, you are doomed for eventual defeat. When there is a weak foundation, the question is not will there be defeat; the question is when will the defeat occur.

It was important for the early church to start out with a strong foundation. After all, she must last until Jesus comes. Therefore, a shallow, narrow foundation would be inadequate for an enterprise that is to last for millennia. A weak foundation would have been a sure recipe for the church to implode centuries ago. In His wisdom, God chose to build His church on the foundation of the apostles with Jesus Christ as the chief cornerstone.

> So then you are no longer foreigners and strangers, but fellow citizens with the saints, and members of God's household, built on the foundation of the apostles and prophets, with Christ Jesus Himself

> as the cornerstone. The whole building is being fitted together in Him and is growing into a holy sanctuary in the Lord, in whom you also are being built together for God's dwelling in the Spirit. (Eph. 2:19–22 HCSB)

The Gospels give us insight into Jesus developing the apostle Peter to be part of the church's strong foundation.

> Andrew, Simon Peter's brother, was one of the two who heard John and followed Him. He first found his own brother Simon and told him, "We have found the Messiah!" (which means "Anointed One"), and he brought Simon to Jesus. When Jesus saw him, He said, "You are Simon, son of John. You will be called Cephas" (which means "Rock"). (John 1:40–42 HCSB)

This first encounter between Jesus and Peter (Simon at the time) is most interesting. Jesus went right to work grooming him to be an apostle and part of the church's foundation. Christ immediately changed his name to "Cephas," which means "rock." At this time he was not even a little pebble, yet Jesus changed his name to "rock." Rocks make strong foundations.

Later in His ministry, Jesus and His disciples traveled to Caesarea Philippi in the northern part of Israel. Here Peter made his famous confession that Jesus was "the Christ, the Son of the living God."

> "And I also say to you that you are Peter, and on this rock I will build My church, and the forces of Hades will not overpower it." (Matt. 16:18 HCSB)

Jesus then declared to the man called "a stone," that He would indeed build His church upon the truth of Peter's statement. Here the Chief Cornerstone of the church speaks to one of the foundation stones of the church about the construction of the church! The church has been building on that foundation ever since. One believer on top of another has been placed into God's holy temple, and the church's foundation is still supporting her today. The church Jesus is building is an impregnable house which even "the forces of Hades will not overpower it" (HCSB).

New Sunday School leaders should start building a strong foundation in their ministry at the outset. A great ministry or class is not built overnight. It is a long process requiring perseverance and commitment. Over time, with a little here and a little there, the stones of the ministry fall in place. The "Sunday School house" built upon a weak foundation will implode; those built upon a strong foundation will become a skyscraper.

Facts about Foundations

Webster's II New College Dictionary defines *foundation* as "the act of establishing; the basis on which a thing stands, is founded, or is supported." Sunday Schools must be built on the foundation of right principles and practices. If not, hurry up and get out of the way because an implosion is coming!

1. The foundation is the most important part of the building.

Builders have told me that people are most interested in the final phases of the building process. They are excited about moving in, smelling the freshly laid carpet, seeing the newly painted walls, enjoying the beauty of the wood trim, and having the pleasure of the newest technology. Builders say that people visit the construction site more as the building gets closer to completion. They also say that owners do not visit the construction site often in the early stages of digging dirt and laying foundations because there is nothing pretty or unusually exciting about slinging dirt!

The analogy fits the church perfectly. We all want to be part of a growing, evangelistic church that is making a difference in her community. We all long for the "finished product" of a healthy, vibrant, exciting ministry. We show up for the services, banquets, and special events because they are appealing. However, not many are around for the dirt-slinging work of laying the church foundation. Sunday School does the nitty-gritty work of the church because she encounters people on a personal basis.

> **Sunday School does the nitty-gritty work of the church because she encounters people on a personal basis.**

2. Foundations are built down in the dirt.

Digging and laying the foundation is dirty work. There is nothing attractive about getting dirty or doing dirty work. People are more impressed with the man in the neatly pressed suit than the one in the grimy overalls. This ditch-digging work is a behind-the-scenes process. It is not on the platform each and every Sunday. It does not usually appear in the weekly church bulletin. Banquets are not held to throw accolades at ditch diggers. Yet this is vital work. Dear Sunday School ditch digger, learn to get your strokes from God.

People bring messes as they have problems, issues, and sin. Sometimes it can get real ugly, but this is the work God has called us to. It is a dirty work and reminds me of the words of Solomon.

> "Where no oxen are, the trough is clean; but much increase comes by the strength of an ox." (Prov. 14:4)

Livestock brings value to the farmer but also drops plops all around the barn. Clean barns require the elimination of livestock that bring profit. So it is with people; they bring

> **Sunday School workers are the pooper-scoopers of the church.**

both value and messes to the church. Somebody has got to help them through their messes and that somebody is Sunday School. Sunday School workers are the pooper-scoopers of the church.

3. Foundations are built with much toil and sweat.

Digging and laying the foundation is not just dirty work; it is also plain old hard work. There is no allurement in sweaty brows, sore backs, and blistered hands. Yet this work accomplishes the most important aspect of the building. This is so true of the church. Some of the most important work of the church takes place down in the preschool Sunday School room where a faithful servant of God builds spiritual foundations in little boys and girls. Next the children's department builds upon this foundation, and then the student ministry develops yet more spiritual formation. In the end we have a tall-standing structure of a mature disciple of Christ who rests on the foundation that was laid way back yonder in those early years by a dear servant of God who showed up every Sunday with a shovel in her hands! We need to understand that blessings are a result of blisters! No blisters, no blessing. A great ministry cannot be built without great workers. There are no shortcuts or magic formulas—just hardworking, hard-hat-wearing, lunch-box-toting laborers.

We need to understand that blessings are a result of blisters!

4. The width, depth, and strength of the building are a direct result of the foundation.

A person planning to construct a large building must prepare large footers. A big building cannot stand on a small foundation. Growing a fruitful Sunday School ministry takes much ditch digging. Sunday School workers must show up each week with a shovel in hand ready to sling some more dirt.

5. Laying a strong foundation takes time, patience, and endurance.

A person planning to grow a great ministry must resolve to stay there awhile. Great ministries come out of the Crock-Pot, not the microwave. Too many people have unrealistic expectations as to what it takes to lay the proper foundation for a great work. Leaders dig deep footers when they properly enlist and train their workers and then see them serve with longevity.

What Are the Foundational Purposes of a High-Definition Sunday School?

There are three foundational purposes of Sunday School—reaching people, teaching people, and ministering to people. Sunday School must accomplish these three things above all else. There are many things that Sunday School can do, but these three things she *must* do. A Sunday School that greatly achieves in other areas but abandons these will eventually implode because the foundational work of the ministry has not been laid. The importance of these three purposes is personified in the ministry of Jesus Himself.

> "Jesus was going all over Galilee, *teaching* in their synagogues, *preaching* the good news of the kingdom, and *healing* every disease and sickness among the people." (Matt. 4:23 HCSB, *emphasis mine*)

Jesus is traveling to the towns and villages around the Sea of Galilee. He is not on a sightseeing tour; He is on a mission that is as visible as a high-definition television. This mission consisted of three purposes.

> **There are three foundational purposes of Sunday School—reaching people, teaching people, and ministering to people.**

- "Preaching the good news"—Jesus was out preaching the gospel, which is evangelism.
- "Teaching in their synagogues"—This was a common practice of Jesus. Luke 4:14–44 gives us great detail of one of those experiences.
- "Healing"—Jesus was always ministering to the hurts and needs of people.

Later in Matthew's Gospel we see Jesus repeating the pattern of this three-fold mission.

> "Then Jesus went to all the towns and villages, *teaching* in their synagogues, *preaching* the good news of the kingdom, and *healing* every disease and every sickness." (Matt. 9:35 HCSB, *emphasis mine*)

We often ask the question, "What would Jesus do?" After reading these two verses in Matthew, we can change this to "What *did* Jesus do?" because the Scripture gives us such a clear picture into His mission. We have correctly been taught that Christians ought to do what Jesus did. I submit to you that Sunday School should also do what Jesus did! Jesus was reaching people, teaching people, and ministering to people. These three purposes form the bedrock foundation upon which we must build our "Sunday School house."

Foundations are to a building what fundamentals are to a sports team. Every coach knows that you must constantly keep working on the fundamentals of the game. As a boy I had a baseball coach who reminded us that we must be able to field a ground ball if we were going to play the game. So every practice he lined up the whole team at third base, and we took turns catching twenty grounders each. Coach told us that he wanted us to stop the ball even if we had to lie down in front of it. This man believed in the basic fundamentals! *Webster's II New College Dictionary* defines "*fundamental*" as "constituting or functioning as an essential component of a system or structure; of major significance."

Facts about Fundamentals

1. Consistently doing the fundamentals separates winners from losers.

Consistency is not doing something nine times out of ten; consistency is doing it ten times out of ten! What if a baseball player caught nine balls out of ten? He would not make it very far. What if our postal mail service only delivered nine out of ten of your letters? What if the doctor only successfully delivered nine out of ten babies? What if airport security only properly screened nine out of ten passengers? It is one thing to do the right thing some of the time; it is an entirely different thing to do the right thing all the time! Sunday Schools certainly do the right thing some of the time; however, we need *constantly* to practice the fundamentals of the Sunday School game. When it comes to achievement, we must be relentless in our pursuit of the fundamentals.

When it comes to achievement, we must be relentless in our pursuit of the fundamentals.

2. Nothing can be sustained until the fundamentals are in place.

Nothing, absolutely nothing, can replace the fundamentals. You can put on high-attendance campaigns, try different curriculum, renovate your facilities, even change to new styles and methods, but until you are disciplined with the fundamentals, all is in vain. Churches are notorious for changing things that do not bring change. A football player can change his uniform, jersey number, position, and even team; but if he cannot block and tackle, he will still be a sorry player. Do not kid yourself to believe you can change your Sunday School for the better without consistently practicing the fundamentals.

What Are the Fundamentals of a High-Definition Sunday School?

Some of these will be discussed at greater length in other chapters, but I want to go ahead and mention them now.

1. Proper Enlistment of Leaders

The significance of proper enlistment of your leaders cannot be overemphasized. If you fail at this point, then the other points have no significance. Our enlistment process is so vague that it leaves the potential worker looking at a fuzzy 1960 television screen instead of a modern high-definition, flat-screen TV. An improper enlistment procedure creates future problems to which we must react. Conversely, a thorough enlistment process proactively abolishes the problem before it gets started. As the great philosopher Barney Fife said, "Nip it in the bud."

2. Quality Training

Research clearly shows that trained leaders are better leaders. In fact, quality training turns a worker into a leader! The more knowledge and skills people acquire, the more empowered they feel. A worker with little knowledge and little skill does not feel confident to lead others. As workers grow, they are now ready to lead others. Hence, they have grown from workers doing tasks to leaders empowered to take others on the journey.

3. Ongoing Sunday School Leadership Meetings

It is imperative that Sunday School leaders meet on a cyclical basis. The work of the ministry must always be planned, coordinated, and tweaked. This cannot happen without a time that is set aside for this purpose. The choir has to meet regularly to plan and coordinate their music. The deacons, committees, and other church entities do the same. So should those leading the most important ministry in the church—Sunday School! It is important to plan the work so you can work the plan.

4. Open Enrollment

We should be constantly enrolling new Sunday School members. We want everyone participating in Bible study. The Word of God is powerful and can bring transformation. Open enrollment simply means that anyone can enroll at anytime. They do not have to be saved or even be church members. At First Baptist Church Woodstock 55 percent of our new members have been previously enrolled in Sunday School when they join the church. If we get them in Bible study, they have a great opportunity to get saved and join the church. In addition, since they are now on the class roll, someone should be calling them and keeping up with them. Fundamentally, we must see Sunday School as an "open door" organization and not a "closed door" society.

5. Starting New Classes

The beauty of starting new classes is that it involves more people in the work of reaching people, teaching people, and ministering to people. Every class must have a leadership base to sustain it. If there are twenty classes, there are twenty people teaching a class; twenty outreach leaders, twenty class secretaries, maybe fifty care group leaders, etc. If there are forty classes, the numbers are doubled, and more laborers are in the field generating twice the harvest.

The purpose of building strong foundations and constantly practicing fundamentals is to avoid failure. Again we look to *Webster's II New College Dictionary* that defines *failure* as "the condition or fact of not achieving the desired end." Failure is a part of life. We all fail, and that is why Jesus came—to deliver us from our failure. We must grasp the reality of experiencing some failures because life will have many. I agree with the old cliché that the road to success is paved with failures. I am not afraid of *failures*, but I am terrified with *failure*. It is OK to have some failures, but we do not want to be a failure. Why? We have only one life in which to win our victories.

Facts about Failure

1. Failure is the cessation of proper execution.

Most Sunday School leaders know what is right and what is wrong. We have the Spirit of God and the Word of God to guide us. Most failure occurs simply because we ceased executing what we know is right. People and organizations fail because they choose not to do what they know they should do.

2. The only difference between success and failure is our willingness to pay the price.

Success is more determined by attitude than anything else. There are some fields where skill plays a more vital role, but the name of the game for success in the Sunday School field is almost entirely one's attitude. This being the case, Sunday School experiences success or failure based on our willingness to make the appropriate decisions and execute the proper fundamentals. Simply put, we must be willing to pay the price.

> **People and organizations fail because they choose not to do what they know they should do.**

3. Time will reveal if we failed.

Many ministries can be deemed successful by the Christian community. However, time will reveal the true success of our ministries. Certainly many of the seven churches of Asia Minor listed in Revelation 2–3 would have been heralded as successful by their generation. Yet Jesus had some words of condemnation to every one of them except the church at Smyrna. In the final analysis God has the final analysis!

What Are the Failures of Standard-Definition Sunday Schools?

Failure will certainly come by neglecting the things listed earlier under "Fundamentals." This would be failure by omission. Failure also occurs by commission; that is, we practice things that are unhealthy for our Sunday School.

1. Closed Curriculum

Closed curriculum is any literature that builds from one week to the next in such a way that would be inappropriate for new people to join a few weeks into it. You cannot practice open enrollment with closed curriculum. The number one task of Sunday School is to reach people, so why would you use a curriculum that discourages people from joining? We want Sunday School to be an "open door" ministry that is "open" each week. There are many great curricula that should be used in closed discipleship groups but not for Sunday School. The only exception would be to start a new class around a subject matter that would draw people not currently in Sunday School. Use this curriculum for one quarter only and then convert the class to an ongoing class using open curriculum and provide them a list of prospects to pursue. Any ongoing Sunday School class that is closed to new people is using rabbit ears for reception instead of high-definition technology.

2. Master Teachers

Some churches have decided that it would be best to take a handful of their best teachers and put everyone into their classes. The rationale is that people would receive the very best teaching available. On the surface this looks good, but this approach has many flaws.

- This approach eventually forces all classes to be large. Some people do not like large classes, and this would discourage them from getting involved.
- This approach diminishes the ability to incorporate different teaching methods. The larger the class the more

a teacher is forced to lecture. Many people are kinetic learners and thrive on personal activity.

- This approach does not develop more teachers. If only the best teach, then no one else is afforded the opportunity to grow as a teacher. Even the great teachers needed time to develop. If a master teacher system were practiced, eventually you would run out of teachers.
- This approach reduces the number of teachers, which reduces the number of classes, which reduces the size of your workforce. There is a trickle-down effect. Limiting the number of teachers ultimately reduces the number of outreach leaders, care group leaders, etc. You take an army and whittle it down to a squad.
- This approach hinders relationship building—the larger the group, the more lecture; the less interaction, the less relationship building.
- This approach is detrimental to people opening up and sharing hurts and needs. The smaller the group, the more open and transparent people are. Conversely, a large class generates people who are less vulnerable. Imagine this scenario: A couple just found out that their teenage son has been smoking marijuana. They are devastated; they are hurting like never before. They come to Sunday School needing friends to put their arms around them, love on them, and pray for them. When the time comes to share prayer requests, they are uncomfortable exposing this to such a large class. So they keep it to themselves. They leave Sunday School that morning carrying the same pain as they entered with because they were never placed in an environment conducive to make this known. Therefore, it is imperative that large classes have time for care groups to meet!

A healthy Sunday School should pursue the three purposes that form the foundation of a high-definition Sunday School, follow the five fundamentals of a high-definition Sunday School, and avoid the two failures of a standard-definition Sunday School. A Sunday School that builds on these principles positions herself for an explosion of growth instead of an implosion.

CHAPTER 3

Keep Evangelism in Sunday School

No area on the Sunday School screen has become more blurry that the area of evangelism. Over time evangelism has seeped out of Sunday School. Evangelism was once the proud purpose and mission of Sunday School. She once served as the front door to the church, and many churches ran a higher number in attendance than did the worship service. Because Sunday School is no longer perceived as the front door of the church, it may also be supposed that Sunday School should not shoulder the responsibility of evangelism. Consequently, the evangelistic tire of the Sunday School has gone flat, not from a blowout but from a small leak. Remember that mission is best accomplished in the context of a small group!

I had a conversation with a minister who stated, "My church is a Great Commission church." I asked, "Is your Sunday School a Great Commission Sunday School?" He said it was not. I then asked, "Is your Sunday School the largest organization in your church?" He said it was. "I have one more question to ask you," I responded. "How can your church be a Great Commission church if the largest organization in your church is not a Great Commission organization?" It amazes me to think that we can have a church actively pursuing the Great Commission when the largest ministry in the church is not!

Every task of a local church must find a way to involve her members actively in those tasks if we expect them to be fulfilled.

Is reaching the lost and unchurched the number one priority that Jesus has for His church? Is it the number one priority of Sunday School? Is reaching the lost and unchurched the number one priority for each Sunday School class? How can a Sunday School be a Great Commission organization if her classes are disengaged in the work of the Great Commission?

There is a trickle-up progression in the work of evangelism. How does a *church* become a Great Commission church? The best way is by pursuing the Great Commission through Sunday School! (Remember that mission is best accomplished in the context of a small group and evangelism is part of the mission.) How does a *Sunday School* become a Great Commission Sunday School? Her classes must be pursuing the Great Commission. How does a Sunday School *class* become a Great Commission class? The teacher leads the class to reach out to the lost and unchurched. It is imperative that classes have leadership that personalizes the call to evangelize and promote the cause for all to be Great Commission Christians. It is one thing for the teacher to exhort the class to be personal witnesses; it is another thing for the teacher to emulate personal evangelism. When it comes to witnessing, more is caught than is taught. Individual Sunday School teachers start an evangelistic succession that works its way up through the class to the Sunday School organization and to the church. Therefore, you grow a Great Commission church one teacher at a time.

How does a *church* become a Great Commission church? The best way is by pursuing the Great Commission through Sunday School!

Why Do Believers Not Witness?

1. We may have become more conditioned by the world than by the Word.

We may have bought into worldly lies to some degree. Over time we have been trained by the world to believe that it is wrong to impose our belief system on others. We are expected to "live and let live." This is not actually exercised by those who perpetuate such a worldview. Our government imposes laws on us that govern driving, taxes, education, smoking, etc. Even moral laws are placed on us such as not stealing, killing, lying, etc. Employers impose regulations on us concerning company policy and job performance. Schools impose restrictions on students concerning academic achievement and even behavioral standards necessary to remain in school. Even those extremists who would rid society of most all laws and regulations are in and of themselves imposing a belief system on us. Imposing no belief system is in itself a belief system.

The Word of God clearly states that we are to be witnesses.

> "Go therefore and make disciples of all the nations, baptizing them in the name of the Father and of the Son and of the Holy Spirit, teaching them to observe all things that I have commanded you; and lo, I am with you always, even to the end of the age." (Matt. 28:19–20)

> "Then the master said to the servant, 'Go out into the highways and hedges, and compel them to come in, that my house many be filled. (Luke 14:23)

> So Jesus said to them again, "Peace to you! As the Father has sent Me, I also send you." And when He had said this, He breathed on them, and said to them, "Receive the Holy Spirit. If you forgive the sins

> of any, they are forgiven them; if your retain the sins of any, they are retained." (John 20:21–23)

This does not give us the right to be ugly or obnoxious, but it gives us the right and responsibility of "speaking the truth in love" (Eph. 4:15).

2. We are fearful.

Many people have a fear of sharing. Many feel rejected by others who do not share their convictions, lifestyle, and worldview. Jesus said we would be rejected, even hated.

> "If the world hates you, understand that it hated Me before it hated you. If you were of the world, the world would love you as its own. However, because you are not of the world, but I have chosen you out of it, the world hates you. Remember the word I spoke to you: 'A slave is not greater than his master.' If they persecuted Me, they will also persecute you. If they kept My word, they will also keep yours. But they will do all these things to you on account of My name, because they don't know the One who sent Me." (John 15:18–21 HCSB)

It is not strange that the world would reject us. As ambassadors of Christ we are His representatives. If the world rejects Christ, then they will certainly reject those who represent Him. The truth is that our fear could be a sign of pride. It may be that our pride cannot handle the rejection. It may be that our pride is fearful that we may be asked something that we do not know the answer.

But whatever our fears may be, they do not provide an adequate excuse for not witnessing. We need to understand the principle that fear is not an acceptable excuse for disobedience! When we stand before God at the judgment seat, will He accept our sin of not witnessing because we were afraid? Some people do not tithe because they are fearful to give 10 percent of their income. Many of these people have a hard time financially making ends meet. Will they be able to stand before God and defend their fear of giving because money was tight or the economy was bad? We cannot excuse our disobedience on fear. If God has commanded it, then, by faith, we are to be obedient.

We cannot excuse our disobedience on fear. If God has commanded it, then, by faith, we are to be obedient.

3. We need training.

Every church should help their congregation know how to share their testimony, or use a gospel tract, and be able to take the Scripture and lead someone to faith in Christ. It is actually not that difficult because the gospel message is simple. Do not operate under the false assumption that some particular evangelism method will save the day for your Sunday School. I have found that if a church has a passion for lost souls, then most any evangelism method will work. The opposite is also true; if a church does not have a passion for lost souls, then it does not matter what evangelism method is used because it will not work! The same can be said for Sunday School classes.

4. We are not in fellowship with the Lord as we should be.

I personally believe this is the greatest hindrance to believers witnessing. Rejection, fear, and lack of training may play into our lack of witnessing a little, but overwhelmingly it is a fellowship issue. Jesus illustrated this well in Luke 15 where He taught a parable using three stories. The first story is about a *lost sheep*. The shepherd had one hundred sheep and one was lost. The shepherd left the ninety-nine sheep to hunt for the one lost sheep. He found the sheep, laid it on his shoulders, and came home rejoicing. He gathered his friends and neighbors and asked them to rejoice with him. The story concludes by stating that there is joy in heaven over one sinner that repents.

The second parable concerns *lost silver.* A lady had lost one of her ten silver coins. After finding the silver coin, she called her friends and neighbors together to rejoice with her. This story concludes as did the first parable, "There is joy in the presence of God's angels over one sinner who repents" (Luke 15:10 HCSB).

The last parable is about a *lost son.* He lives in sin and wastes the inheritance received from his father. One day he sees the error of his ways, repents, and comes home. His father has been anxiously looking for him and throws a party.

In Luke 15 everyone is happy; everyone is rejoicing, both those on earth and those in heaven. Well, everyone except big brother. He is not happy because he is out of fellowship with his father! If he were properly aligned with his father, then he would love what his father loved, and his father loved baby brother coming home! This illustrates that our lack of witnessing has little to do with all outward barriers and obstacles; it's an inside job! We are not right with the Father. If we were, we would love what He loves, and He so loves the world that He gave His only begotten Son! Above all else, the greatest thing we can do to become soul winners is to get in right fellowship with our heavenly Father.

A few additional thoughts concerning Luke 15 promote soul winning.

- Notice the diligence of the shepherd. Luke 15:4 says, "What man among you, who has 100 sheep and loses one of them, does not leave the 99 in the open field and go after the lost one *until he finds it*?" (HCSB). We do not know how long it took the shepherd to find the sheep. We do not know how far he had to travel to find the sheep. We do not know the rough terrain or the bad weather he had to endure. We do know that he was going after that lost sheep with great determination and was going to do what ever was necessary to find it. The last four words of verse 4 say much, "until he finds it."

- Notice the thoroughness of the woman to find her lost silver coin. Verse 8 says that she was diligently seeking her coin. She was not taking a casual approach like an Easter egg hunt. She was consumed in finding her lost coin. Notice that the last four words attached to her search are, like the shepherd, "*until she finds it*." There was a resolve in her search that would only end when she found her coin. The shepherd and the woman had to employ two different methods. The shepherd was in the open, out in the fields. The woman was in the house. The issue was not their surroundings, their environment, or the method they used. Their passion and diligence made the difference! Evangelism is more about the motive than the method, the spirit than the scheme, and the tenacity than the technique!
- The lesson of the lost son is not an account of a backslidden Christian coming back to the Father. It is a descriptive teaching of salvation. Three points to this perspective: first, note the audience Jesus is addressing. Luke 15:1 says, "Then all the tax collectors and the sinners drew near to Him to hear Him." Jesus wasn't teaching believers; He was teaching lost people. Why would Jesus be teaching lost people about how a backslidden Christian ought to come back to God? If you had a roomful of lost people and had the chance to speak to them, would you teach them about how a backslidden Christian ought to come back to God? Of course not, it would be inappropriate and have no point of reference or application with them. Second, I want you to notice the word "parable" in verse 3. It is used in the singular, not the plural. A parable is an earthly story with a heavenly meaning. In Luke 15 we have three earthly stories with one heavenly meaning. The fact that *parable* is used in the singular indicates that all three stories have a singular

meaning and application. Therefore, the third story of this chapter must be congruent with the first two stories. Third, the language used is salvation language.

> "This son of mine was dead and is alive again; he was lost and is found." (Luke 15:24 HCSB)

> "It was right that we should make merry and be glad, for your brother was dead and is alive again, and was lost and is found." (Luke 15:32)

- The whole time little brother was gone, his elder brother remained on the farm with his father, yet he did not catch his father's heart for his lost brother. Big brother was with his father often but somehow missed the great passion of his father's heart. Likewise, do we sit and hear Bible lessons week after week and never catch our Father's heart? Are we content to do our chores on the farm but never see our Father's great passion for the world? May God give us ears to hear what the Spirit is saying to us!

5. We lack a church strategy.

Sunday School is the church's strategy to reach lost and unchurched people! What good is a sermon if there is no strategy to implement its truths? Sunday School gives the church a practical way to collectively pursue the Great Commission. How does a church go after a couple in their thirties that becomes interested in spiritual issues? How does a church reach out to high school students who need Christ? How does a church reach that couple who just got married or those median adults who just moved into the community? With our age-appropriate Sunday School classes!

> **Sunday School is the church's strategy to reach lost and unchurched people!**

Individual Sunday School classes form a natural connection for the church's outreach strategy and assimilation strategy. The people reaching prospects will be the same ones building relationships with them, and relationships are the best assimilation tool the church has. Every class ought actively and aggressively to pursue people who would be in their class if they attended because this aligns our outreach strategy with our assimilation strategy. Sunday School is the assimilation arm of the church so she should also be the outreach arm of the church. The way you reach them is the way you keep them.

Reaching people is an ongoing process. Oftentimes we reach out to a prospect with a visit or phone call, and then that prospect never hears from us again. Essentially we have implemented a hit-and-run outreach strategy. We hit them with the gospel, and then they never hear from us again. Now, let me be quick to say that this is better than never hitting them with the gospel. However, it is usually an ineffective way to reach them. Most people are not going to respond to a gospel message or an invitation to church from a person they have just met for the first time. People today are skeptical and need to have a trust level with the messenger before they buy in to his message. Therefore, outreach must be seen as a process, a relationship-building process. The ones who should build that relationship are those in their life stage, which would be someone in their prospective Sunday School class. This is the reason we have implemented the MTV strategy at First Baptist Church Woodstock.

This strategy provides an easy way to employ continual "touches" on the prospect that will help build a relationship. When a class receives a prospect, we ask them to make an initial visit. After the initial visit we ask them to follow up each week thereafter with sequential contacts of Mail, Telephone, and Visit. The "touches" on the prospect look like this:

- Week 1: Make initial visit.
- Week 2: Mail them a note (can be e-mail).
- Week 3: Telephone them.
- Week 4: Visit them again.

If we still have not gotten them connected, then we continue the Mail, Telephone, Visit cycle over and over again until we do get them connected in Sunday School or they instruct us to leave them alone. The MTV strategy gives every class a hands-on, practical way to carry out the church's mandate to be Great Commission people. It also gives every person a means by which they can get involved in reaching others. Some will not be comfortable making a visit, but they might be comfortable writing a note or making a phone call.

Along with the MTV strategy there are other strategic actions a class can implement to obey the Great Commission. These actions are simple, basic, and doable so everyone can have some part in helping the class reach others.

- Each class weekly participates in outreach visitation. The class can be represented each week at outreach visitation. It can be the same team of two to three people each week, or the class can implement rotating visitation teams that have one week a month.
- Each class births a new class. By starting new classes, we put more people to work. It expands the organization so we have more teachers, outreach leaders, care group leaders, etc. The more laborers we put in the harvest fields, the more produce we will reap.
- Each adult class sends out members to serve in the preschool, children, and youth departments so they can expand their organization as well.
- Classes move to a different Sunday School hour to open up space at the dominant hour is a way a class can participate in the Great Commission. When we provide additional space for others, then we are partaking of the church's mission to reach others.
- People parking off campus and riding a shuttle to the church campus is another way we can be active in the Great Commission. Allowing visitors to have a place to

park is part of the Great Commission. Visitors will not attend a class or worship service if they can't park their car.

All of these things are so simple and so achievable. These small acts contribute to the great cause of the Great Commission. It is not that hard because these actions require more attitude than skill. It just takes a little thought and a little sacrifice on our part. If Jesus could go to Calvary to die for the sins of others, surely we can park off campus, teach children, or move to another hour. We can all do something that makes a tangible contribution to the mission Christ gave to us.

Adult Class Outreach Leaders

It is extremely important that each class have an outreach leader. The class teacher already has much responsibility without taking on additional tasks. The outreach leader should coordinate and direct the class's outreach efforts in reaching her prospects. Prospects are gathered from those who have visited our worship service or Sunday School, participated in our recreational leagues, attended special church events, helped through our benevolent ministries, etc. These prospects are distributed to classes that match their age and marital status. Our outreach leaders are given ten minutes every week during the Sunday School class time to do three things.

- Distribute prospect cards for the purpose of follow-up by mail, telephone, or visit. It also provides a time to retrieve any cards that need to be turned back in.
- On a monthly basis have someone in the class share a testimony. People who can share their testimony before the class can share it with a class prospect. This provides a great practice field. Hearing a testimony of someone's salvation experience also fuels the evangelistic fire of others. When you listen to others share how they got saved, it prompts you to want to see other people saved.

- Each adult class is asked to form a Strategic Mission Partnership (SMP) with a foreign missionary. This partnership entails the class praying for the missionary and going to his part of the world to help him with his work. Classes raise their own support to do this. I am thrilled to report that we have hundreds of Sunday School members all over the world in a year's time. Jesus cast the vision of winning the world when He gave us the Great Commission. He then gave us the strategy by which to accomplish it in Acts 1:8. Adult class outreach leaders lead their classes to be involved in "our" Jerusalem and around the world. They serve as the class "Acts 1:8 strategist."

Personal Evangelistic Responsibility

The church has forgotten to use Sunday School as her evangelistic arm and as a result baptisms decrease every year. The cold, hard fact is that we are seeing fewer people saved every year! We preach evangelism, and we have the good intention of wanting to see people come to Christ, but we have removed the personal responsibility of every believer to be a witness. Evangelism floats around in the domain of the theological and philosophical but never finds its way to the practical. We need to be reminded that Jesus said, "Go, ye" not, "Go ya'll." Any Christian who is not purposefully, specifically, and intentionally witnessing and trying to reach lost and unchurched persons is not in the will of God! I did not say they were not good church members; I did not say they were poor citizens; I did not say they were not good neighbors or employees. I said they were not in the will of God. How can we say we are in the will of God when we ignore the last thing He told us to do? The Great Commission was a command spoken to individual Christians, not the corporate church. The church is merely a composite of her individual members. Therefore, every Sunday School member should be challenged to find some way to participate in the Great Commission.

Today it takes forty-seven Southern Baptists to win one person to faith in Christ in a year. The number of Southern Baptists needed to win one person to Christ in 1954 was sixteen. What's the difference? There are many contributing factors, but it cannot go unnoticed that we have removed evangelism from Sunday School. Sunday School is now relegated to accomplish two things: Bible study and fellowship. Both of these are certainly worthy to be pursued by every Sunday School class. Who would not want to attend a class that did not practice these two valuable endeavors? However, these two, standing alone, represent a shortsighted vision for Sunday School.

We need to be reminded that Jesus said, "Go, ye" not, "Go ya'll."

Many Sunday Schools are no longer promoting or actively pursuing the Great Commission. Our Sunday Schools are imploding because we have removed evangelism from her to-do list. A Sunday School cannot expect to explode with growth if she is not purposefully implementing the Great Commission into her DNA. Sunday School *is* the outreach arm of the church so we must keep evangelism in Sunday School. It is time we put evangelism back on the big high-definition screen of Sunday School because nothing will infuse your Sunday School with energy like seeing people saved!

CHAPTER 4

Teaching Content with Intent

The greatest job in the world is preaching. I am not referring to a vocational position at the church that requires the delivery of a sermon every week to a congregation. I am talking about proclaiming the gospel of Jesus Christ to lost and dying people. I think the apostle Paul had this in mind when he penned Romans 10.

> On the contrary, what does it say? The message is near you, in your mouth and in your heart. This is the message of faith that we proclaim: if you confess with your mouth, "Jesus is Lord," and believe in your heart that God raised Him from the dead, you will be saved. With the heart one believes, resulting in righteousness, and with the mouth one confesses, resulting in salvation. . . . For everyone who calls on the name of the Lord will be saved. But how can they call on Him in whom they have not believed? And how can they believe without hearing about Him? (Rom. 10:8–10, 13–14 HCSB)

It is no wonder Paul concludes by saying those who proclaim the gospel have beautiful feet.

> And how shall they preach unless they are sent? As it is written: "How beautiful are the feet of those who preach the gospel of peace, who bring glad tidings of good things! (Rom. 10:15)

Those who preach the gospel proclaim the message of eternal life to others. Jesus instructed Peter of this at Caesarea Philippi after he proclaimed Jesus as "the Christ, the Son of the living God" (Matt. 16:16).

> "And I also say to you that you are Peter, and on this rock I will build My church, and the forces of Hades will not overpower it. I will give you the keys of the kingdom of heaven, and whatever you bind on earth is already bound in heaven, and whatever you loose on earth is already loosed in heaven." (Matt. 16:18–19 HCSB)

The second greatest vocation in the world is teaching. Teachers communicate knowledge; they bestow wisdom; they add value; they give potential; they build futures; and they impart life! In fact, teachers have the unique privilege of participating in the two greatest vocations there are!

The important ministry of a Sunday School teacher cannot be overstated! Teachers handle the two most precious things to God every week—God's Word and God's people. I do not know of anything God loves more than His Word and His people. Churches need to understand the significance of their Sunday School teachers. All teachers need to understand the significance of their ministry in the lives of their class members. Teachers have an exalted place in the church!

Teachers handle the two most precious things to God every week—God's Word and God's people.

Over the years I have observed teaching that falls short of it's intended purpose. Teachers understand their role to instruct people with biblical knowledge and facts. They comprehend the need to study and to handle the text with great accuracy. They know they must represent the truth at all cost. This is most commendable. However, teachers must go a step further because they are more than just teachers; they are leaders. They lead those they teach. Their teaching platform also presents a leading platform. Because they are the keepers of truth, they naturally become the leaders of those they teach. Teachers can be compared with pastors. They have a platform to proclaim, "Thus saith the Lord." Their preaching platform also gives them the privilege to lead the church. It is the principle of osmosis as the teaching and preaching ministries gradually absorb the platform to lead.

Jesus taught us truth that profoundly impacts a teacher's ultimate goal, which is to produce obedient Christians.

> "If you love Me, you will *keep* My commandments" (John 14:15 HCSB, *emphasis mine*)

Notice that Jesus did not say, "If you love me, *know* my commandments." The acid test of our love for Christ is not how much Bible we *know* but how much Bible we *obey*! What is obedience? It is the act of carrying out a command. A few verses later Jesus reemphasizes this thought again.

> "The one who has My commands and *keeps* them is the one who *loves* Me. And the one who *loves* Me will be loved by My Father. I also will love him and will reveal Myself to him." (John 14:21 HCSB, *emphasis mine*)

Again, I call your attention to the fact that love was expressed to Jesus not through knowledge but through obedience. Jesus is hanging on this idea for effect. He wants to get His message through, and He wants to make sure we are getting it, so He brings attention to this great truth one more time.

> Jesus answered, "If anyone loves Me, he will *keep* My word. My Father will love him, and We will come to him and make Our home with him." (John 14:23 HCSB, *emphasis mine*)

Three times Jesus presents this truth. I would call this "truth in HD." Jesus is trying to sharpen our focus on the reality of love. He wants to make sure we see this truth with great clarity. Apparently the apostle John clearly saw this truth because he also recorded it in 1 John 5:2–3.

> This is how we know that we love God's children when we love God and obey His commands. For this is what love for God is: to keep His commands. Now His commands are not a burden. (HCSB)

Sunday School teachers should teach for the sake of obedience and not just for the sake of knowledge. Imparting knowledge is certainly needed because people cannot be obedient to that of which they are ignorant. We must teach to impart knowledge, but we must not stop there. Teachers have got to see this truth with a sharp focus. Leading people to obey must be to be the focus of every lesson. If it is not, then we may contribute to the sinfulness of the people we teach.

Sunday School teachers should teach for the sake of obedience and not just for the sake of knowledge.

> "Therefore, to him who *knows* to do good and *does not* do it, to him it is sin." (James 4:17 NKJV, *emphasis mine*)

Next to this verse in my Bible I have written, "Wow! Woe!" I am wowed by this truth because it challenges our thinking. It is easy to think that we are right just because we have the right understanding of a passage, but James, the half brother of our Lord, presents a spiritual fact that repeatedly goes unnoticed. He did not say that if we know to do good and do bad it is sin. He said that knowing to do good and doing nothing is sin! That is, to have biblical understanding of the commands of the Bible and not actively pursue obeying them is sin. This, my friend, is a "woe." Just think of the ramifications of that truth. Each week a Sunday School teacher presents a Bible lesson to class members that hear and understand the commands of God. They then go home and do nothing about it. Our teaching just made a greater sinner out of the Sunday School member! If we have knowledge of the good commands of God and do not apply them to our living, then we are made a greater sinner according to James 4:17. Not to contribute to the sinfulness of class members, teachers must exhort application of biblical truth. Do not misunderstand me; a teacher can only do so much, but should it not grieve the heart of any Bible teacher to see no spiritual growth in the lives of his class members? Should it not burden him seeing his class members not be faithful to worship, to read their Bibles, to love and serve others, to exercise their spiritual gifts, to tithe, to witness, etc., after hearing lesson after lesson on these commands? Should it not motivate the teacher to do all he can to help people apply God's Word? We are only right when we think right and do right!

If we are to produce Great Commission Christians (The Bible study ministry of the church ought to do that.), then we must obey the teachings of Christ. Below is the Great Commission with two words omitted; see if you can find the two words I left out.

> And Jesus came and spoke to them, saying, "All authority has been give to Me in heaven and on earth. Go therefore and make disciples of all the nations, baptizing them in the name of the Father and of the Son and of the Holy Spirit, teaching them all things that I have commanded you and lo, I am with you always, even to the end of the age. (Matthew 28:18–20, *intended word omission*)

These two words are critical if we are to correctly understand and interpret this important passage. The ramifications of just two words dramatically change the application of Jesus' command. The two words are "to observe." Jesus said, "Teaching them *to observe* all things that I have commanded you." If Jesus had said, "Teaching them all things that I have commanded you," then we would teach only for the sake of dispensing content. The teacher's job would be to lift the lid of people's brain, regurgitate biblical facts and data until their brains were full, close the lid, and send them on their way. When you add "*to observe* all things that I have commanded you," then you throw a whole new meaning on the verse. We are now to teach them biblical content with the intent of leading them to obedience! Our content is no longer a stand-alone activity; our content now has intent. Dietrich Bonhoeffer said it well, "One act of obedience is better than one hundred sermons."

Our content is no longer a stand-alone activity; our content now has intent.

Obedience is essential in being successful. Like it or not, success is dependent upon playing by the rules, not just knowing the rules. People are in prisons today because they refused to play by the rules. Any recipe for success includes the willingness to follow instructions. Spiritual success is no different. One simple work of obedience will release more of God's power into our lives than a thousand sacrifices. This is a lesson that

King Saul had to learn the hard way. God had told him to annihilate completely the Amalekites and their animals.

> "Thus said the LORD of hosts: 'I will punish Amalek for what he did to Israel, how he ambushed him on the way when he came up from Egypt. Now go and attack Amalek, and utterly destroy all that they have, and do not spare them. But kill both man and woman, infant and nursing child, ox and sheep, camel and donkey.'" (1 Sam. 15:2–3)

Saul decided to keep the best of the animals and only destroy those that were unwanted.

> "But Saul and the people spared Agag and the best of the sheep, the oxen, the fatlings, the lambs, and all that was good, and were unwilling to utterly destroy them. But everything despised and worthless, that they utterly destroyed." (1 Sam. 15:9)

The Lord then sent Samuel, the prophet, to confront Saul with his disobedience.

> So Samuel said, "When you were little in your own eyes, were you not head of the tribes of Israel? And did not the LORD anoint you king over Israel? . . . Why then did you not obey voice of the LORD? Why did you swoop down on the spoil, and do evil in the sight of the LORD?" And Saul said to Samuel, "But I have obeyed the voice of the LORD, and gone on the mission on which the Lord sent me, and brought back Agag king of Amalek; I have utterly destroyed the Amalekites. But the people took of the plunder, sheep and oxen, the best of the things which should have been utterly destroyed, to sacrifice to the LORD your God in Gilgal." So Samuel said: "Has the LORD as great delight in burnt offerings and sacrifices, as

> in obeying the voice of the Lord? Behold, *to obey is better than sacrifice,* and to heed than the fat of rams. (1 Sam. 15:17, 19–22, *emphasis mine*)

Saul thought he would please God by taking some of the animals he spared and sacrifice them to God. He quickly found out that God was not nearly as interested in his sacrifices as He was his obedience. Samuel then taught Saul just how terrible disobedience is.

> "For rebellion is as the sin of witchcraft, and stubbornness is as iniquity and idolatry. Because you have rejected the word of the Lord, he also has rejected you from being king." (1 Sam. 15:23)

Willfully rebelling against the command of God is equated with witchcraft. To be stubborn in disobeying the Lord is an iniquity likened unto idolatry. Can the Scripture be any more plain about the seriousness of knowingly disobeying the revealed will of God? Therefore, we are compelled to teach our content with intent.

Obedience must come even without the benefit of understanding.

Obedience must come even without the benefit of understanding. Saul may have thought that it would be prudent to keep the good animals. They would provide labor in the fields, food for the table, and sacrifices to God. God said otherwise. Jesus also challenged Peter to obey without understanding.

> Then He got into one of the boats, which was Simon's and asked him to put out a little from the land. And He sat down and taught the multitudes from the boat. When He had stopped speaking, He said to Simon, "Launch out into the deep and let down your nets for a catch." But Simon answered

> and said to Him, "Master, we have toiled all night and caught nothing; nevertheless at Your word I will let down the net." And when they had done this, they caught a great number of fish, and their net was breaking. (Luke 5:3–6)

Peter did not understand Jesus' command. Being a professional fisherman, he knew this was not the correct way to catch fish. However, Peter obediently stated one important word that we cannot overlook, "nevertheless." In essence Peter said, "Lord, I do not understand. This makes no sense to me, but nevertheless I will." Peter's obedience did not require his understanding. He wanted to understand, but he obeyed in spite of his understanding. What a great truth and lesson we need to share. Many spouses feel distant from their mate. They no longer have that loving feeling, but God's command is one man and one woman till death do them part. Even though they do not understand or do not feel like it, they need a "nevertheless" in their vocabulary. We need to comprehend that God has obligated Himself to bless nothing but our obedience! He has not promised to bless our intelligence, looks, personality, charisma, etc. He only blesses obedience.

The big challenge for all teachers is moving their people from being "hearers of the Word" to "doers of the Word." This is no easy or simple undertaking. There are no magic formulas or secret keys that unlock this dilemma. It is a continuing process requiring patience, longsuffering, and much trial and error.

On the day of Pentecost the Holy Spirit came and filled the believers. They began to speak in other languages so that those gathered from all over the world could hear the gospel of Jesus Christ. As these unlearned believers spoke in languages they did not previously know, many questioned this strange phenomenon asking, "Whatever could this mean?" (Acts 2:12). The apostle Peter then preached the death, burial, and resurrection of Jesus Christ. After the message, those that had previously asked, "What does this mean?" now asked,

"What shall we do?" (Acts 2:37). The Scripture then records Peter's counsel and the result.

> Then Peter said to them, "Repent, and let every one of you be baptized in the name of Jesus Christ for the remission of sins; and you shall receive the gift of the Holy Spirit." . . . Then those who gladly received his word were baptized; and that day about three thousand souls were added to them. (Acts 2:38, 41)

The teacher is greatly helped by following the pattern of Peter in responding to the two questions posed him in Acts 2. We should move people from *what* the Scripture means to *how* to apply them.

From *What*	To *How*
(Acts 2:12)	(Acts 2:37)
Apathy	Acknowledgement
Curiosity	Commitment
Interest	Involvement
Mediocrity	Missional
Unbeliever	Believer

The teacher should help people understand "what does this mean?" so that they would want to know "what shall we do?" Here are some defining words that will help teachers understand actions they need to undertake to help people move from hearing to doing.

"What Does This Mean?"	"What Shall We Do?"
Articulating	Applying
Conceptualizing	Coaching
Describing	Doing
Exhorting	Emulating
Explaining	Expecting
Proclaiming	Practicing

Jesus gave us a great example to follow as a teacher who had content with intent.

> Then He appointed twelve, *that they might be with Him* and that He might send them out to preach, and to have power to heal sicknesses and to cast out demons. (Mark 3:14–15, *emphasis mine*)

Jesus' method of teaching was not exclusive to talking. The one and true Master Teacher spent time with His disciples so that He could model truth for them. He did not just tell them; He took them. Sunday School teachers should follow Christ's example and do class ministry projects by going together to witness, visit hospitals, meet people's needs, etc. The teacher can personify biblical truth to his class members as they do ministry together.

Society's approach to learning today is very passive. I believe television has fostered noninteractive, nonthinking students and the entertainment industry has conditioned us to sit and receive. We are asked to do very little or even to contemplate anything. Our only responsibility is to turn the television on and then be fed. It seems that when entertainment was radio and reading, we had more creative, imaginative, and involved learners. Progression in technology seems to have produced regression in thinking. Today's Bible teacher must recognize the dilemma that many people who sit in their class have become passive receptors. Therefore, drawing people out of their passive comfort zone is a challenge for any teacher and yet should be the goal of every teacher. Teachers cannot be satisfied with class members showing up merely to watch or be entertained. We must lead them to be discoverers and examiners of biblical teachings.

We must adhere to the principle that maximum involvement equals maximum learning. Everyone should be engaged in the learning process. I have always felt that the greatest thing I could do for my class was to get them to think for themselves. God gave them a mind for a reason. If I could engage them in the learning aspect of the Bible, I always felt my chances of engaging them in the doing aspect of the Bible were greatly enhanced.

We must expand this principle and realize that maximum involvement equals maximum learning, and maximum learning equals maximum obedience. When people discover truth for themselves, they are more apt to obey that truth. Of course, the opposite is true. A lack of involvement produces a lack of learning. Spoon-fed truth is not often digested. Therefore, using a variety of methods becomes a must for every teacher. Everyone does not learn the same way. As more methods are used, more people can connect with the lesson. As members connect, they become more interested, more involved, and consequently, more obedient.

> **We must adhere to the principle that maximum involvement equals maximum learning.**

After our church went to a new Sunday morning schedule, it provided an hour of Sunday School where there was no worship service. This gave Pastor Johnny an opportunity to attend Sunday School so he visited some Sunday School classes with the goal of joining one. (He did join one and is in Sunday School every week.) One day in a staff meeting he shared about visiting classes and said to me, "Allan, we have some wonderful classes, and we have some teachers who really know their Bibles, but I have noticed that many of them lecture every week. I think we want to get people interacting in a Sunday School class." "I agree, Pastor, we do want people interacting in Sunday School," I replied, "and I think I know why so many teachers lecture and where the problem lies. Pastor, you are the problem." Now at this point I was going to have some fun or many regrets! Pastor grinned and said, "All right, tell me more." I then explained that it was really a compliment to him. He was such a great Bible teacher, a wonderful communicator of truth, and so passionate about the Word of God that all the teachers wanted to be like him. When teachers hear the Word proclaimed, they most always hear it preached from the pulpit. Unconsciously their mind is conditioned that preaching or lecturing is the way to do it. They mimic that style in their Sunday School class. We must be careful that we do not turn Sunday School into an age-division worship service. Sunday School is to be distinctly different from a worship service.

As we involve people, not only do they learn more effectively, but their retention rate increases as well. Retention is a by-product of concentration. Therefore, teachers cannot afford to let class members sit on the sidelines each week and watch the teacher play the game. They must be engaged in the game with the teacher. Members discovering truth are involved; involvement produces concentration; concentration produces retention; retention means they have grasped a truth. They are positioned to obey because they understand. It is shameful for the teacher to take "the word of God [which] is living and powerful, and sharper than any two-edged sword" (Heb. 4:12) and render it dead, weak, and duller than a butter knife to the unengaged member.

THE GROWTH OF SUNDAY SCHOOL IN HD

---

growth: the process of growing; an increase, as in size (*Webster's II New College Dictionary*)

CHAPTER 5

The Two Rules of Winning

Every church that has a small group ministry desires that ministry to thrive instead of just survive and to take new territory, not just to hold on to what you have. Yet every report I have read in the last few years indicates that is not the case. Sunday School is not growing; it is declining. Some have suggested that Sunday School is outdated, irrelevant, and antiquated. I disagree! Is studying the Bible irrelevant? Are caring and ministering to a small group antiquated? Is reaching out to others outdated? Are building relationships and fellowshipping with other believers no longer needed? I cannot understand those who say Sunday School is no longer germane.

On the other hand, I cannot escape the fact that Sunday Schools are no longer as vibrant as they once were. The facts cannot be ignored, so the questions must be posed. Is it because Sunday School is no longer effective, or have we rendered it ineffective? I believe the latter. Again, reaching lost and unchurched people is the great need of the church, and Sunday School can do it! Teaching people the truths of the Word of God is essential, and Sunday School can do it! Ministering to the many needs of people is ever increasing, and Sunday School can do it! Developing meaningful relationships that add value to one's emotional health is vital, and Sunday School can do it!

I think we would all agree that our Sunday Schools should be exploding with growth; however, I am of the opinion that they are declining, not from growing outdated and useless but from an implosion. You see, it is an inside job. We are crumbling from within. We have forgotten the essentials of the game. With all the changes that have taken place over the years in the game of football, one thing has remained a constant, that is, you do not win if you do not block and tackle! Over the years Sunday School has undergone some changes and will continue to do so, but the basics to a vibrant Sunday School are still intact. I want us to sharpen our focus on the two essential rules of winning.

Over the years Sunday School has undergone some changes and will continue to do so, but the basics to a vibrant Sunday School are still intact.

- First Rule of Winning: Don't beat yourself.
- Second Rule of Winning: Practice the fundamental disciplines of the game.

The two rules of winning are life principles; they apply to all aspects of life. They apply *individually.* Many people today are beating themselves. The world is not beating them, the system is not beating them, and even Satan is not beating them. They are self-destructing. Each person must incorporate some simple, fundamental disciplines into his lifestyle in order to be successful. The Bible has much to say about having a work ethic, guarding your tongue, managing your finances, treating people appropriately, etc. These two rules of winning abound in scriptural teaching.

The two rules of winning apply *organizationally.* Organizations, like individuals, cannot ignore basic management principles and expect to stay afloat. Their existence is halted by a self-inflicted wound. Sunday School is no different. Sunday Schools that practice the first rule of winning will not experience a self-inflicted *implosion.* Sunday Schools that practice the second rule of winning will see a growth *explosion.*

Sunday Schools that apply these two rules are capable of an *explosion* which *Webster's II New College Dictionary* defines as "a sudden and great increase." If we are not defeating ourselves and are practicing the fundamental disciplines of Sunday School, then it stands to reason that an increase is coming. When we adhere to the two rules of winning, we minister with great expectation and anticipation because something is about to break loose.

Natural Principles/Process of Growth

Jesus seemed to indicate that a natural growth process operates on a cause-effect principle.

> And He said, "The kingdom of God is as if a man should scatter seed on the ground, and should sleep by night and rise by day, and the seed should sprout and grow, he himself does not know how. For the earth yields crops *by itself*: first the blade, then the head, after that the full grain in the head, But when the grain ripens, immediately he puts in the sickle, because the harvest has come." (Mark 4:26–29, *emphasis mine*)

It is assumed that the natural principles of growth are operative here. Seed is placed in the soil where the rain and sunshine eventually bring forth the growth process of blade to ear, to a full ear of corn. Jesus said the "earth yields crops *by itself*." The Greek word is *automatos* from which we get *automatic*. When natural growth principles exist, automatic developments occur.

Fruit is the natural product in this cause-and-effect cycle. We all want fruit; we all want a thriving Sunday School. We give great attention to the effect. Our problem is that little focus is given to the cause. If we want to be healthy, we must work on the cause that produces that effect. When we neglect the cause, then the effect will be rotten fruit instead of luscious fruit. Notice, Jesus said that a man should cast seed. This seed starts the cause-and-effect cycle that later produces the blade, then the ear, and then the full corn in the ear. You see, there is a natural cause-and-effect cycle that explodes with new corn. If we are to experience a fruitful Sunday School, then we must cast forth the seeds (cause) that will ultimately bring forth a harvest (effect).

Some say Sunday School no longer works, when in reality, we quit working Sunday School! Any garden will grow weeds. You cannot plant a garden and then leave it unattended. Bugs, animals, and weeds will consume an unattended garden, and when the garden becomes unmanned, you are beating yourself. Any process, practice, or program left to itself will regress to an unhealthy state. A healthy, fruitful Sunday School requires constant attention. The Sunday School garden will yield a great crop if we properly care for it.

Some say Sunday School no longer works, when in reality, we quit working Sunday School!

I have often wondered how many Sunday Schools are self-defeating. Like the garden, they have been unmanned, unattended, and consequently, unproductive. The devil does not have to beat them or oppose them because they are killing themselves. Consider this letter from Satan.

A Letter from the Devil

> Dear Sunday School Members,
>
> I visited your Sunday School last Sunday and was overjoyed to see so many of you had not attended. I become very anxious when I see people participating in Bible study. That's why I have so many fun activities to keep you out late on Saturday nights.
>
> I heard some lessons not well prepared, so much of your allotted time for Bible study was consumed

in discussing ball games and business concerns. Furthermore, many classes reported no contacts for the week. Absentee members and class prospects were completely ignored; boy does that ever make me feel good! When people's needs are met and people genuinely care about one another, it makes things hard for me. You are doing such a wonderful job of fellowshipping with one another that you have no time for anyone else. You are making my job so easy that I may take four weeks vacation this year instead of my usual two.

Also, I noticed the loneliest place in town on outreach night is the church. I always sweat this night out because if you go out and tell someone about Jesus, they just might get saved. That is the worst news I could receive! But you Sunday School people are so easily turned away by other important priorities that my staff and I plan for you. I have discovered that your convenience is more important to you than your mission.

Well, I just wanted to drop you a note and encourage you to keep up the mediocrity. No sense in your getting all worked up about this gospel stuff anyway. Why, people will begin to think you are a fanatic if you do.

In conclusion, let me say that I'm always here to assist you. If anyone starts putting pressure on you to become a fully committed disciple, rooted and grounded in the Word, and more involved in the Great Commission, just let me know. I have a pit full of excuses.

Your friend for all eternity,
Satan

Self-Defeating Sunday Schools

A self-defeating Sunday School violates the first rule of winning. Here are a few ways we beat ourselves.

1. Biblical Liberalism

Any church or any class that does not believe in an inerrant, infallible, inspired Bible is doomed for failure. Why would anyone want to attend a Bible study where the teacher did not believe in the Book from which he was teaching? We are saved by faith, and our faith is dependent on the integrity of the Word of God. An eternal faith must come from an eternal Word. If the promise upon which our faith rests is not valid, then neither is our faith.

> So then faith comes by hearing, and hearing by the word of God." (Rom. 10:17)

Why do we have a legitimate faith? We have it because we have a legitimate Word from God. An incorruptible faith can only come from an incorruptible seed. A watered-down Bible can produce nothing but a watered-down faith. A faulty Bible can only produce a faulty faith; but an incorruptible Word produces an incorruptible faith.

> Having been born again, not of corruptible seed but incorruptible, through the word of God which lives and abides forever, because "All flesh is as grass, and all the glory of man as the flower of the grass. The grass withers, and its flower falls away, but the word of the LORD endures forever." (1 Pet. 1:23–25)

The standard for the Word of God is set in our churches first by the pastor and then by the teaching ministry of the church, which is the Sunday School. People are not going to attend church if leaders do not have an unwavering confidence in the Book they are preaching and teaching.

2. Too Much Concentration on Felt-need Curriculum

I believe in a systematic, process-driven, exegetical approach to Bible study. Why? It is the best way to process spiritually healthy disciples of Christ. I think there is a place for some felt-need curriculum, but it should be used as an appendage to your systematic study of all of God's Word. People do need courses on marriage, parenting, finances, etc., but often, classes get so enamored with a particular topic that they become unbalanced. There are varying thoughts on what should dictate your curriculum choices.

- The curriculum should be dictated by those we are trying to reach.

Those with this viewpoint want to use their Sunday School to reach the unchurched, so they set their curriculum to do just that. This is not a bad thought. In fact, I appreciate the desire to reach those outside the church walls. However, you still have those within the walls that need to be discipled.

- The curriculum should be set by those in the class.

This perspective says that we ought to minister the Word to those who are already here. This is a justifiable argument to grow those currently in the class. The class would find out the needs of those attending and set a curriculum map to address those needs.

- The curriculum should be set by God.

This is my approach. I am not trying to be more spiritual than others, but I really do believe that God, and God alone, ought to set the teaching agenda! It is His Word, we are His people, and it is His church, so allow Him to drive this decision. I believe God has already set the teaching agenda for the church when He gave us His Word complete with sixty-six books. Why are Haggai, Micah, Amos, and Philemon in the Bible? God wanted us to have them and to study them. Surely God knew what He was doing when He placed them in His Holy Book! This is why I believe every church ought to have a systematic approach to study the entirety of Scripture. Do we need occasionally to have a topical study? Yes, we do. But I believe our bread and butter ought to be an exegetical, systematic curriculum that walks us through the entire Bible. I believe this was the teaching of Jesus Himself.

> But He answered and said, "It is written, 'Man shall not live by bread alone, but by *every word* that proceeds from of the mouth of God.'" (Matt. 4:4, *emphasis mine*)

As we study systematically through the Bible, we will meet the needs of the unsaved and unchurched. Similarly, an exegetical Bible study approach will address the discipling needs of the saved. We can take great confidence that the God-breathed Word will do its own work as we are faithful to read and study it. The writer of Hebrews recorded that the Word of God is a two-edged sword.

> For the word of God is living and powerful, *and sharper than any two-edged sword*, piercing even to the division of soul and spirit, and of joints and marrow, and is a discerner of the thoughts and intents of the heart. (Heb. 4:12, *emphasis mine*)

Why did the inspired writer refer to the Word as a "two-edged sword"? I cannot be sure, but my sanctified imagination tells me that the two edges are evangelism and discipleship. As the teacher takes his class through a systematic, exegetical study of Scripture, he finds that it cuts evangelism into unsaved members of the class, and at the same time, it cuts discipleship into the believing members of his class. The Word of God is not inadequate or insufficient but is alive and powerful.

3. A De-emphasis on Sunday School

Some churches today are de-emphasizing Sunday School. By simply ignoring it, they allow it regressively to fade away. They quit working the "Sunday School garden" permitting it to be overtaken by weeds and animals. Many of them will then proclaim that Sunday School does not work in our contemporary world. Others want to pursue a new model. This may be appropriate in some settings, but I am concerned when it appears that pride is driving the issue. I suggest this because some feel they must do something other than that which is traditional. Every tradition is not necessarily good, but every tradition is not necessarily bad either. The issue to me is not whether something is traditional or not; the issue is whether it is effective or not. The "Sunday School garden" will still produce an abundant harvest when its soil is worked. We have a right to say that Sunday School does not work only after we have worked it and found it unproductive. Any small group method will prove unproductive when little labor is exerted on it. Every farmer knows that fruit is the product of hard labor.

> **The "Sunday School garden" will still produce an abundant harvest when its soil is worked.**

4. Pastor's Overinfatuation with the Worship Service

Notice I said *over*infatuation with the worship service. A pastor should be infatuated with the worship service. Worship is important and vital because worship is clearly commanded in Scripture. God demands our worship, deserves our worship, and desires our worship. Furthermore, pastors should want to preach (God help the church where he does not want to!). My point here is not to minimize worship and preaching. My goal is to strike a balance in the way a pastor leads the church. Pastors should promote worship and expect members to attend and participate in worshipping God. Pastors should also be infatuated with Sunday School, because Sunday School is the body of Christ at work doing the mission of the church and interacting with other believers.

5. Sunday Schools That Meet for the Sake of Meeting

Sunday School must have a purpose that is greater than just meeting so we can say we met. Time is the precious commodity of our day. People have more to do than just attend for the sake of attending. Sunday School has three purposes that are to reach people, teach people, and minister to people. Each purpose should be incorporated into each class on purpose. We must know our purpose and then purposefully execute the purpose! Sunday Schools need to know their purpose and then be tenacious in their pursuit of it. When Sunday School becomes nothing more than a social club, it will die for lack of a transcendent cause.

6. Sunday School is for the Sole Purpose of Bible Study and Fellowship

Many Sunday School leaders believe that Sunday School is about Bible study and fellowship. While this is true, it is shortsighted. Sunday School is a great place to visit friends and socialize with those who share a similar worldview that is Bible based. It is also a place where the saints of God are mobilized to carry out the commission of Christ. You see, Sunday School is social and relational, but she is also missional! We must embrace evangelism if we are to be a Great Commission Sunday School, and we must accept the responsibility of ministering to people's needs. We often relegate Sunday School to Bible study and fellowship because that is mostly what takes place in the classroom on Sunday morning. Evangelism and ministry are often overlooked because they function outside of the Sunday morning classroom. We naturally gravitate toward that which is easier and more convenient. We naturally drift away from that which takes more effort and labor.

Sunday School is social and relational, but she is also missional!

7. Sunday School That Has No Standard for Leadership

In many churches there is only one criteria to be a Sunday School leader, and that is you must have a pulse! In my book *The Six Core Values of Sunday School*, I state, "My philosophy of a Sunday School class is: The class is a miniature congregation, and the teacher is a miniature pastor." That being the case, a "miniature pastor" must meet criteria that exceed just having a pulse. We must have godly, committed people leading and shepherding our classes. When you drive the success of Sunday School down to the lowest common denominator, you find it one class at a time. A Sunday School organization is only as good as the contribution of each individual class. When we take that one step further, we find that the success of the class is the teacher. Therefore, we need teachers who will toe the leadership line if we are to have a healthy, growing Sunday School ministry.

Knowledge Versus Willpower

Some Sunday Schools implode for lack of knowledge, but not many. Most implode from a lack of will. They simply beat themselves. Sometimes we are lazy, lack focus, or do not prioritize, but the result is the same—a losing Sunday School. Why do football teams get beat? Sometimes they do not practice and prepare as they should; sometimes they focus on other things; sometimes it is not the priority it should be. The result is senseless penalties like jumping offsides, lining up wrong, or senseless mistakes such as fumbling the ball, making the wrong read, or poor execution like using the wrong technique, dropping the pass, missing the tackle, etc. The bottom line is that the other team did not have to beat them because they beat themselves! As a former high school football coach, this used to drive me nuts! I could somewhat handle it if we played our best and got beat because all you can do is your best. If we did not play our best and got beat . . . well, it was ugly!

Jesus teaches us a great principle in Luke 6:46–49:

> "But why do you call Me 'Lord, Lord,' and not do the things which I say? Whoever comes to Me, and hears My sayings and *does them*, I will show you whom he is like: He is like a man building a house, who dug deep and laid the foundation on the rock. And when the flood arose, the stream beat vehemently against that house, and could not shake it, for it was founded on the rock. But he who heard and *did nothing* is like a man who built a house on the earth without a foundation, against which the stream beat vehemently; and immediately it fell. And the ruin of that house was great." (*emphasis mine*)

What was the difference between these two men? The Bible says nothing of their skills, talents, IQ, personalities, charisma. In fact, Jesus said that they both *heard*. The difference is that one heard Jesus' sayings and *does them*; the other man *did nothing*. The difference was not knowledge, because they both heard. The difference was one did and the other did not! The last man in the parable violated the first rule of winning! Sunday Schools fail when their leaders choose not to do what they should do. I submit to you that those leading declining Sunday Schools probably know the same basic fundamentals as those leading growing Sunday Schools; they just do not execute them! They have not the will to do what they know they should do. Many of you can now put the book down and go to work because you have gotten what you needed. The rest of you keep reading.

CHAPTER 6

Timing Is Everything

Timing is everything. There was a perfect time when God decided to invade the world with His incarnate Son. Our all-knowing God sent Jesus at the exact time in the history of mankind.

> But when the *fullness of the time* had come, God sent forth His Son, born of a woman, born under the law. (Gal. 4:4, *emphasis mine*)

God is a God that is on time. He is never early and He is never late. He shows up "when the fullness of time had come." He came to redeem us when the time was right, and He will return for us when the time is right. He will be on time as it pertains to His will and way. We may think He should have already acted or that He may need to act now, but He will act in His perfect time. He is not held captive by our time schedules or circumstances. Yet He is always with us through our every trial.

God is a God of timing. Sometimes God says yes, sometimes God says no, and sometimes He tells us to wait. If you are like me, you can take the yes and the no better than His answer to wait. He occasionally chooses to put us on a divine holding pattern like a pilot who has not been given the go-ahead to land. God did this with Mary and Martha.

Now a certain man was sick, Lazarus of Bethany, the town of Mary and her sister Martha. . . . Therefore the sisters sent to Him, saying, "Lord, behold, he whom You love is sick." When Jesus heard that, He said, "This sickness is not unto death, but for the glory of God, that the Son of God may be glorified through it." Now Jesus loved Martha and her sister and Lazarus. So, when He heard he was sick, He stayed two more days in the place where He was. . . . These things He said, and after that He said to them, "Our friend Lazarus sleeps; but I go that I may wake him up." Then His disciples said, "Lord, if he sleeps he will get well." However, Jesus spoke of his death, but they thought that He was speaking about taking rest in sleep. Then Jesus said to them plainly, "Lazarus is dead. And I am glad for your sakes that I was not there, that you may believe. Nevertheless let us go to him." . . . So when Jesus came, He found that he had already been in the tomb four days. . . . Now Martha said to Jesus, "Lord, if You had been here, my brother would not have died." . . . Then, when Mary came where Jesus was, and saw Him, she fell down at His feet, saying to Him, "Lord, if You had been here, my brother would not have died." . . . And some of them said, "Could not this Man, who opened the eyes of the blind, also have kept this man from dying?" Then Jesus, again groaning in Himself, came to the tomb. It was a cave, and a stone lay against it. Jesus said, "Take away the stone" Martha, the sister of him was dead, said to Him, "Lord, by this time there is a stench, for he has been deal four days." Jesus said to her, "Did I not say to you that if you would believe you would see the glory of God?" Then they took away

> the stone form the place where the dead man was lying. And Jesus lifted up His eyes and said, "Father, I thank You that You have heard Me. And I know that You always hear Me, but because of the people who are standing by I said this, that they may believe that You sent Me." Now when He said these things, He cried with a loud voice, "Lazarus, come forth!" (John 11:1, 3–6, 11–15, 17, 21, 32, 37–43)

God's timing was right and His timing was best.

God is an on-time God. He rescued Daniel from the lions' den right on time. He rescued the three Hebrew children in the fiery furnace right on time. He calmed the sea for the fearful disciples right on time. He pulled Peter from drowning right on time. He miraculously delivered Peter out of the prison right on time. He called Saul of Tarsus on the road to Damascus to take the gospel to the Gentile world right on time.

God is a God who understands time. Jesus testified, "I must work the works of Him who sent Me while it is day; the night is coming when no man can work" (John 9:4). Benjamin Franklin once said, "Do not squander time, for that is the stuff life is made of." Time is the raw material of life. Our numbered days will soon be gone for the "night is coming when no man can work." So, use your God-given days wisely. Be employed in that which is fruitful for the kingdom. Remember, you have enough time every day to do God's will, but you may not have enough time to do both God's will and your will. May we follow the advice of the apostle Paul who instructed the churches at Ephesus and Colossae to "redeem the time" (Eph. 5:16; Col. 4:5).

As we can see, both time and timing are important. Every leader must consider not only the right thing to do but also the right time to do it. Many would say that *now* is the right time to do the right thing. However, there are times when the right timing is not now. Martha, Mary, and the crowd in John 11 certainly thought that Jesus should have showed up earlier. They felt He could have done the right thing by healing Lazarus, but He showed up too late. Timing has a great impact on success or failure. I know a Sunday School leader who implemented a Sunday School covenant at the wrong time that resulted in a church fight and dismissal of a staff member. He did a good thing, but he implemented it at the wrong time. Doing the right thing requires conviction; doing it at the right time requires wisdom. The Bible records events where wisdom in timing was applied. The men of the tribe of Issachar understood the times and what Israel ought to do during these times.

> Of the sons of Issachar who had understanding of the times, to know what Israel ought to do. (1 Chron. 12:32)

Rehoboam, Solomon's son, certainly did not have the wisdom of his father. He forsook the wisdom of Solomon's elderly advisers to lighten the tax burden on the people. Instead, he followed the advice of his generation and it resulted in ten of Israel's twelve tribes leaving his kingdom. As the new king, he did not understand the timing of his decision, and it cost him 83 percent of his kingdom. Timing is important!

> Then Solomon rested with his fathers, and was buried in the City of David his father. And Rehoboam his son reigned in his place. And Rehoboam went to Shechem, for all Israel had gone to Shechem to make him king. . . . that they sent and called him. Then Jeroboam and the whole assembly of Irael came and spoke to Rehoboam, saying, "Your father made our yoke heavy; now therefore, lighten the burdensome service of your father, and his heavy yoke which he put on us, and we will serve you." So he said to them, "Depart for three days, then come back to me." Then King Rehoboam consulted the elders who stood before his father Solomon while he still lived, and he said, "How do you advise me to answer these people?" And they spoke to him, saying, "If you will be

> a servant to these people today, and serve them, and answer them, and speak good words to them, then they will be your servants forever." But he rejected the advice which the elders had given him, and consulted the young men who had grown up with him, who stood before him. And he said to them, "What advice do you give? How should we answer this people who have spoken to me, saying, 'Lighten the yoke which your father put on us'?" Then the young men who had grown up with him spoke to him, saying, "Thus you should speak to this people who have spoken to you, saying, 'Your father made our yoke heavy, but you make it lighter on us'—thus you shall say to them: 'My little finger shall be thicker than my father's waist! 'And now, whereas my father put a heavy yoke on you, I will add to your yoke; my father chastised you with whips, but I will chastise you with scourges!'" . . . Now when all Israel saw that the king did not listen to them, the people answered the king, saying: "What share have we in David? We have no inheritance in the son of Jesse. To your tents. O Israel! Now, see to your own house, O David!" So Israel departed to their tents. But Rehoboam reigned over the children of Israel who dwelt in the cities of Judah. (1 Kings 11:43–12:1, 3–11, 16–17)

The book of Esther records an amazing story when Queen Esther's uncle, Mordecai, challenged her to go into the king without being asked, even though it was against the law. He realized the timing was imperative if Israel was going to be saved from annihilation at the hands of wicked Haman. Timing is everything!

> And Mordecai told them to answer Esther: "Do not think in your heart that you will escape in the king's palace any more than all the other Jews. For

> if you remain completely silent *at this time*, relief and deliverance will arise for the Jews from another place, but you and your father's house will perish. Yet who knows whether you have come to the kingdom *for such a time as this*?" Then Esther told them to reply to Mordecai: "Go, gather all the Jews who are present in Shushan, and fast for me; neither eat nor drink for three days, night or day. My maids and I will fast likewise. And so I will go to the king, which is against the law; and if I perish, I perish!" So Mordecai went his way and did according to all that Esther commanded him. (Esther 4:13–17, *emphasis mine*)

The Right Time to Start a New Sunday School Year

Typically most churches start a new Sunday School year sometime in late summer or early fall. Churches like to coincide the Sunday School year with the public school start. I am of the opinion that this is the best time. Families are back at home and vacations are over. In my county public schools usually start the first Monday in August. Therefore, our church starts our new Sunday School year the first Sunday in August. Children do not like to be a fourth grader at school and remain in the third grade Sunday School class. They feel belittled. I want to start the year off with enthusiasm, energy, and momentum.

> **Consider some timing issues that every Sunday School leader must contemplate.**

The argument has been made that it is better to begin at the quarterly break of the curriculum. Certainly this is a valid point. The thought is that the particular course of study can be completed and the transition to a new class, new teacher, and a new curriculum can all be made at once. The Sunday School leader has to make the decision as to what is best for his Sunday School. The principle that drives my decision on this issue is that people are more important than curriculum! That being said, let me tell you what I did not say. I did not say that people are more important than truth. I did not say that people are more important than God's Word. I would rather base my decision on what is right for the people over what is right for the curriculum. Why? The curriculum is to serve the people not vice versa. Sunday School is in the people business, not the curriculum business. A common thought is that people are always to succumb to certain principles, but we also need to be reminded that people are the principle thing. This was the lesson that Jesus had to teach the Pharisees.

> Now it happened that He went through the grainfields on the Sabbath; and as they went His disciples began to plunk the heads of grain. And the Pharisees said to Him, "Look, why do they do what is not lawful on the Sabbath?" But He said to them, "Have you never read what David did when he was in need and hungry, he and those with him: how he went into the house of God in the days of Abiathar the high priest, and ate the showbread, which is not lawful to eat except for the priests, and also gave some to those who were with him?" And He said to them, "The Sabbath was made for man, and not man for the Sabbath. Therefore the Son of Man is also Lord of the Sabbath." (Mark 2:23–28)

We often need to remind ourselves of the priority. What is the main thing? Jesus had to help the Pharisees with their perspective. I believe the right perspective is that people trump curriculum. Curriculum is important, needed, and useful; but people are even more important, needed, and useful. Jesus died for people, not curriculum!

The Right Time to Have Sunday School Leadership Meetings

Every church should have regular, ongoing Sunday School leadership meetings. Every Sunday School teacher and leader should attend those meetings. Part of a church's enlistment process should include a commitment from the potential teacher to attend the Sunday School leadership meetings. (I say much about this in *The Six Core Values of Sunday School*). The question is often asked, "When is the best time to have these meetings?" This will differ from church to church, but a guiding principle should be followed, and that is to conduct Sunday School leadership meetings at the time conducive for the best attendance. At First Baptist Church Woodstock, we hold a monthly meeting on the third Sunday afternoon of the month. Some churches have a weekly meeting each Wednesday night. Some hold meetings either before or after the Sunday morning activities. Do not, I repeat, do not allow other activities to dictate your meeting. If you do, then you violate the principle of conducting Sunday School leadership meetings at the time conducive for the best attendance.

In this book I am attempting to make a case for the importance of Sunday School and how vital it is to a local church. If this is the case, then leadership meetings need to take place at the time when her leaders can best meet because they are leading the charge to reach people, teach people, and minister to people. These leaders are the ones making the most important ministry in the church happen! Therefore, they need to be given a premium spot on the church calendar!

An overwhelming number of churches would consider Sunday morning as "Prime Time A" because this is when the largest number of people attend church. "Prime Time B" is usually Sunday night or Wednesday night depending on which time draws the most people. It may be another time for a few churches. Typically Sunday morning, Sunday night, and Wednesday night make up the Prime Time A, B, and C.

Imagine that at Local Community Church Sunday morning is Prime Time A; Wednesday night is Prime Time B; and Sunday night is Prime Time C. The church leaders at Local Community Church meet to decide how to distribute her ministries across the church calendar. They decide the following.

- Prime Time A (Sunday morning)—Worship and Sunday School
- Prime Time B (Wednesday night)—Discipleship ministry, choir practice
- Prime Time C (Sunday night)—Committee meetings and Sunday School leadership meeting

The thought process is that the Discipleship ministry should be granted Prime Time B, not the Sunday School leadership meeting. I respectfully disagree with that perspective. Most churches are fortunate to have 33 percent of their Sunday morning attendance participating in a discipleship class. Should we not make the teaching and discipling time more effective when it is touching the masses in Sunday School? It seems appropriate to put our discipleship eggs in the Sunday School basket.

The problem with the arrangement of time and ministries at Local Community Church is that the Sunday School leadership meetings are positioned for failure. They are given the worst time slot on the church calendar. Later we will deal with some growth principles, but one rule must be stated now: Sunday morning rules! If Sunday morning rules, then those making Sunday morning happen ought to get priority seating on the church schedule and calendar. I recognize that other factors may be involved and each church must make those decisions, but it is in the best interest of the church to adhere to these guiding principles as much as possible.

I think it is in the best interest of Local Community Church to situate the Sunday School leadership meetings on the schedule at Prime Time B slot. The church's growth is more directly affected by the effectiveness of Prime Time A than any other thing. I want to be prepared for Prime Time A; therefore, I will use Prime Time B to support it.

The Right Time to Start New Classes

I love starting new classes so much and have such a passion for it that I am tempted to say anytime is a good time to start a new class. However, my zeal may outrun my better thinking. Starting new classes should be done at times that are conducive for them to experience success. Most new classes cannot overcome immediate failure. Therefore, it is best to start new classes at peak attendance times of the year. In most churches it would be detrimental to start classes during the summer when people are vacating and traveling. Holiday seasons are times to avoid as well.

Starting new classes should be done at times that are conducive for them to experience success.

Many churches experience peak attendance after school starts and late winter/early spring. Whatever the peak seasons are at your church is the time to projcct thc starting of new classes. It places the new classes in a successful environment. For example, expectant parents work hard to prepare their home so they can place their newborn in a home that is favorable for growth and healthiness. They maintain a clean home and rid the home of anything dangerous and harmful to their baby. Birthing a new class needs to carry the same care and attention. You want that newborn class to be healthy, to grow, and to reach her God-given potential.

The Process of Teacher/Class Maturation

Like people, classes need time to mature. Typically classes do not begin with great teaching, great outreach, and great ministry. These things take time. As leaders, our job is to train class leaders with the right philosophy and tools so they can start the process of pursuing the goal set before them. We are naïve to expect these things to develop quickly. If we expect too much too quickly, then we set ourselves up for much frustration. Furthermore, we destroy the morale of the class leaders who will come to believe that they are asked to do the impossible. I have seen this happen to the point that lay leaders have lost trust in their leader. They felt the leader was a "little Hitler" who was building his own kingdom with little regard for the soldiers on the front lines. At the same time, we err if we do not have expectations of both the goal to pursue and a reasonable amount of time in which to accomplish it.

The Sunday School leader walks the tightrope on many fronts and this is one of them. If the leader has no expectations, then he falls off one side of the tightrope. If his expectations are too unreasonable, then he falls off the other side of the tightrope! Welcome to the world of Sunday School leadership! It takes great wisdom and balance to stay on the Sunday School tightrope. Leaders should think through a reasonable process of class maturity and understand that the maturity of the class is directly tied to the leadership maturation of the teacher.

> **It takes great wisdom and balance to stay on the Sunday School tightrope.**

I believe strongly in the three tasks of Sunday School: *reach people*, *teach people*, and *minister to people*. I also believe strongly that mission is best accomplished in the context of a small group. I try to let my principles guide my decisions. I was in a meeting with our adult education team and our missions department. We embraced the idea that our worldwide mission endeavors should be funneled through our Sunday School classes because mission is best accomplished in the context of a small group. There was no need to invent another small group organization when there was one already in place. The decision was made to implement our Acts 1:8 strategy of taking the gospel from "Woodstock to the World" through individual Sunday School classes. We had just started a third Sunday School hour with fifty-two new classes. In our meeting the discussion came up about how we could get these new classes involved in a Strategic Mission Partnership (SMP). I was uncomfortable with pursuing this with our new classes because we had just birthed them; they were not ready for this kind of ministry yet. They had not developed as a class to the point that they could handle this. Like a child, they needed time to mature.

I wanted to expose them to our philosophy and direction on this, but I did not want to put pressure on them to embrace an SMP immediately. Remember, class maturation is directly linked to the maturation of the teacher, and all of these teachers were brand new. In the meeting I went to the dry-erase board and drew a diagram of the "Cycle of Teacher Maturation."

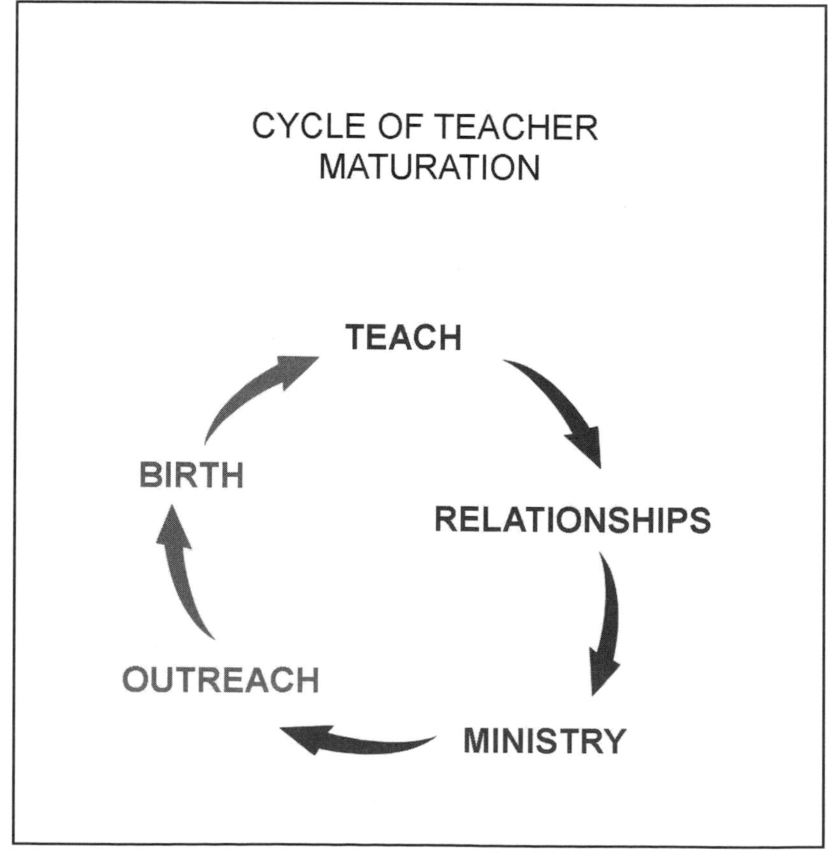

The Sunday School leader needs to understand that a new teacher has one thing on his mind. He wants to know how in the world he is going to get a lesson together for Sunday! We can talk foreign missions, local outreach to our community, birthing new classes, ministering to people's needs, etc., all we want, but Sunday is coming! All teachers want to perfect the art of teaching because they have to stand before a group of people for thirty minutes each week and deliver the goods. The greatest fear people have is public speaking. We want them to be good teachers, and they want to be good teachers, but until they feel comfortable with their ability to teach, they will do little in regard to other tasks their class is asked to pursue. This is reality! The Sunday School leader needs to help the teacher teach before we ask the teacher to lead. Competency is the teacher's great ally in helping people believe and trust in him. If the class recognizes him as a good teacher, they will be more apt to follow him in the other tasks of the Sunday School as well.

The second item on the teacher's agenda is building relationships with those in the class. It is natural to want to know those whom you are teaching and leading. Small groups of people are bent toward relational interaction even in secular settings. Furthermore, teachers will be most effective leading their class to grow, reach out, and birth a new class when they lead from relationship rather than position. The first two steps in the Cycle of Teacher Maturation gain teachers the confidence and followership of their class members because they are now led by his competency and relationship.

Once relationships are established, the teacher will naturally want to see his members' needs met. Innate within us is the desire to help those whom we know and love. I suggest that the teacher start developing care groups in his class at this point and involve others in the caring ministry of the class. The teacher cannot do everything, so he must expand his leadership by producing more leaders in the class.

Up to this point in our Cycle of Teacher Maturation everything that has been a priority all takes place within the four walls of the classroom. Now that these issues are resolved, the teacher, and consequently, the class, can start reaching out and becoming more missional. At this point the class should be developing a list of prospects to cultivate. An outreach leader should be enlisted who will first lead the class to reach their prospects and then embrace the Acts 1:8 strategy of establishing a Strategic Mission Partnership outside of their own community.

As outreach and growth occurs, the class is now postured to birth a new class and start the cycle all over again. Each generation reproduces another generation as they mature from infant to adult. As classes mature along with their teacher, they should reproduce also. I am of the conviction that the newly birthed class can grow through the maturation cycle quicker than the mother class if the mother class has been effective in understanding and implementing the purposes of Sunday School. The new class has been exposed to the teaching and example of maturity much like a child can mature quicker when he is raised and exposed to mature parents.

The Right Time for Momentum

The question is often posed, "How does Sunday School get momentum going?" It is always the right time to have momentum, but getting it can be a great challenge. The better question is, "How do you build morale into your teachers?" Momentum is the cumulative of teacher morale. The collective morale of your individual teachers equals the amount of organizational momentum you have.

The collective morale of your individual teachers equals the amount of organizational momentum you have.

The Sunday School leader *creates* momentum one teacher at a time. This means the leader is always working on teacher morale. Morale is established as the leader relates to the teacher. It starts in the enlistment process, carries over into Sunday School leadership meetings, and is further propelled through ongoing, individual interactions. The leader should make himself as accessible as possible to his teachers. Look for ways to touch your people and especially use times of church gatherings.

My mom, who loves humor, told me a story about the German general who was trying to create momentum with his troops toward the end of World War II. It was becoming apparent that they were going to lose the war, and morale was low. To make matters worse, his troops had been on the battlefield for weeks with little food and rest and had not had a bath or a change of clothes in weeks. Needless to say they needed a pick-me-up. So, being the good leader that he was, the general decided to inspire his troops. He gathered them together one morning and said, "Soldiers, I have some bad news and good news today." They responded, "Give us the good news first; we have had enough bad news." So the general gleefully shouted, "Gentlemen, we are getting a change of underwear today!" Shouts of cheer and thunderous applause were heard with laughter and dancing. Finally, as the soldiers rejoicing subsided, one asked, "General, what is the bad news?" The general replied, "Schmidt, you change with Schultz!"

I doubt the general created the momentum he had hoped for, but at least he knew it was needed and was his responsibility to provide it. We often think we need to be a great motivational speaker if we are to inspire people. Certainly this is an effective means, and we should all develop and improve this aspect of our leadership, but I want to offer three simple yet effective ways to inspire people.

I try to follow the three *A*s in building morale. The first is *attention*. Giving people attention is powerful in connecting with them because people like to be noticed. When you give someone attention, you communicate, "I like you; I value you; you are significant." When you do not give them attention, you convey, "I don't like you; I don't value you; you are not significant." How do I know this? This is exactly how I feel when people give me attention or fail to do so.

Some may defend themselves claiming that they really do value people, but they are shy or not very outgoing, etc. This may be true, but it does not lessen the perception of the one feeling ignored. Leaders simply cannot afford to be inattentive to people. What are leaders in business to do? Lead people. You best lead people by relating to them. When they know you, they will want to follow you and will be pleased that you are their leader.

The second *A* is *affirmation*. When you see or hear good things about your people, then affirm them for it. When you affirm right behaviors, you reinforce the repetitiveness of those behaviors. A handwritten note, a phone call, or catching them in the hallway at church will all provide a means for you to express your gratitude for a job well done. Affirmation is to a person what gasoline is to a fire. People become even more ignited for the work and in the work when someone notices! Trust me, leader, people notice when you notice.

The third *A* is *appreciation*. Everyone wants to be appreciated for their contribution and sacrifice. I know their motive for serving is to honor the Lord and serve Him, but even a dog needs a pat on the head occasionally. As a teenager I remember my pastor, Thomas Gatton, often saying, "Give people their roses while they can smell them." Since I purchased my home, it has increased in value, and that is called "appreciation." My car, clothes, and furniture have decreased in value since I purchased them, and that is "depreciation." As a leader, I want my people to rise in value; therefore, I *appreciate* them. As they rise in value, they become more valuable!

Your Sunday School will only be as valuable as the leaders running it. So make them more valuable. As they become more valuable, they have greater morale, and as their morale rises, so does your organizational momentum! Leaders only succeed when others want them to. Do your workers want you to win? If not, you will end up a tired, frustrated, defeated, and unsuccessful leader. If your workers do want you to win, you will have great friends, team camaraderie, and great momentum with your work.

The Sunday School leader must then *capture* momentum by celebrating successes with his teachers. There are two strategic ways the leader can use his Sunday School leadership meetings to capture momentum. One is to share points of celebration like a class that has reached a new family in the community or a care group that has greatly ministered to a hurting family. A second way is to recognize a "Teacher of the Month." As you brag on the teacher to your people, you lift her to another level. She will now do even more for the class than before and will also serve as a model and example to the other teachers.

Your Sunday School will only be as valuable as the leaders running it. So, make them more valuable.

The leader then must *continue* momentum by using it like a snowball rolling down the hill gaining more snow as it rolls. Momentum is too hard to acquire to let it easily slip away. Continuing momentum is best accomplished by starting new classes from your successful ones. Observe the classes doing well and work with them on starting new classes. Thriving classes generally replicate other success stories because once you have tasted success, you never want to go back.

What time is it, leader? It is time to build a great Sunday School team that is on mission for God! Therefore, the Sunday School leader must aspire to inspire until he expires!

CHAPTER 7

Producing Reproducers

The greatest thing a Sunday School can do to infuse energy and vitality into the organization is to see lives changed and people saved. The second greatest thing it can do to inject life into the organization is to reproduce new leaders. New leaders birth new life, new thoughts, and new enthusiasm into the ministry. The new air provided by new leaders breathes freshness into a stale organization.

Webster's II New College Dictionary defines *reproduce* as "to produce a counterpart, image, or copy of; to produce again." Jesus must have had this in mind when He gave us the Great Commission. Paul certainly had this in mind when he instructed Timothy on how to lead the church.

> And what you have heard from me in the presence of many witnesses, commit to faithful men who will be able to teach others also. (2 Tim. 2:2 HCSB)

If we are seeing Sunday School clearly, we will understand the need of the Sunday School to continually reproduce leaders. A Sunday School in HD will be ingrained with this mind-set. Reproduction is not just the job of the church staff but of every Sunday School teacher and leader. Reproducing more leaders is a monumental task and requires all hands on deck. If the Sunday School leader is the only person producing more leaders, then the ministry is in serious trouble. With this in mind, let me answer several questions about reproducing.

Who Should Reproduce?

All born-again believers in Christ should be reproducing themselves as they lead others to faith in Christ. We should spiritually procreate as we beget others in Christ Jesus. Jesus Himself gave His disciples some rich teaching on this subject.

> "I am the true vine, and My Father is the vineyard keeper. Every branch in Me that does not produce fruit He removes, and He prunes every branch that produces fruit so that it will produce more fruit." (John 15:1–2 HCSB)

Who Can Reproduce?

Everyone *should* reproduce, but not everyone *can* reproduce because only those abiding in Christ *can* reproduce. As reproducers we are dependent on Him rather than independent from Him.

> "Abide in Me, and I in you. As the branch cannot bear fruit of itself, unless it abides in the vine, neither can you, unless you abide in Me." (John 15:4)

Who Can Reproduce Reproducers?

It is one thing to reproduce yourself; it is a different thing to reproduce reproducers. How can we not only produce fruit but also produce reproducers who produce more fruit?

> "Every branch in Me that does not bear fruit He takes away; and every branch that bears fruit He prunes, that it may bear *more* fruit. . . . I am the vine,

> you are the branches. He who abides in Me, and I in him, bears *much* fruit; for without Me, you can do nothing. . . . By this My Father is glorified, that you bear *much* fruit; so you will be My disciples." (John 15:2, 5, 8, *emphasis mine*)

Notice how Jesus spoke of producing *more* fruit, then moved to producing *much* fruit. Jesus seemed to signify that there is another level a branch can go to in its reproduction process. Let me go ahead and tip my hand on this. When a branch is purged, it can "bring forth more fruit." That is, when the branch is pruned it is posed to reproduce "more fruit." Sunday School applies this biblical principle to her ministry by birthing new classes from our existing classes. As a class releases others to start new classes, others are dispersed into the producing business.

Can Everyone Produce the Same Amount?

Not everyone can produce equally because we have different gifts and abilities. Our goal is not to match the production of others; it is to maximize our own God-given potential. Each of us ought to possess an attitude that causes us to pour into others. We should each strive to reproduce ourselves and to help develop others as if they had to take our place. This is true of Sunday School classes. It should not be expected that every class match each other in producing the same amount of fruit. However, it should be expected that every class produce something and reach their God-given potential.

It should be expected that every class produce something and reach their God-given potential.

Why Reproduce?

When we reproduce, we "stir up the gift of God" in others. We arouse the gifts and abilities that lie dormant in others, and we put into motion the gifts bestowed upon them by the Holy Spirit.

> Therefore I remind you to stir up the gift of God which is in you through the laying on of my hands. (2 Tim. 1:6)

Everyone serving in a local church always needs additional help. There is always a demand for additional servants. When we reproduce more workers, we support those already serving. Laborers strengthen one another and multiply one another's ministries.

> Two are better than one because they have a good reward for their efforts. For if either falls, his companion can lift him up; but pity the one who falls without another to lift him up. Also, if two lie down together, they can keep warm; but how can one person alone keep warm? And if somebody overpowers one person, two can resist him. A cord of three strands is not easily broken. (Eccles. 4:9–12 HCSB)

By reproducing, we better serve one another because more and various kinds of gifts are now operative within the body. As others join in serving, they supply what may have been missing. A team of workers helps to supplement one another's giftedness.

> Now as we have many parts in one body, and all the parts do not have the same function, in the say way we who are many are one body in Christ and individually members of one another. (Rom. 12:4–5 HCSB)

As laborers multiply, the church grows spiritually and numerically. A healthy church will be experiencing both kinds of growth.

> And He Himself gave some to be apostles, some prophets, some evangelists, and some pastors and teachers, for the equipping of the saints for the work of ministry, for the edifying of the body of Christ, till we all come to the unity of the faith and of the knowledge of the Son of God, to a perfect man, to the measure of the stature of the fullness of Christ. (Eph. 4:11–13)

God receives glory when we reproduce. As we reproduce more laborers, we produce more fruit which brings glory to God.

> "By this My Father is glorified, that you bear much fruit; so you will be My disciples." (John 15:8)

Why Do We Not Reproduce?

We do not reproduce because we are not intentional.

We learned in chapter 1 that good intentions alone are no better than no intentions unless we get intentional about our good intentions! We know to reproduce, but we never get intentional about it. How many Sunday School classes have a plan to start new classes? The answer will indicate the intentionality of your Sunday School. One does not fall into success; one must climb up to success. Therefore, classes must identify the mountain of reproduction and start climbing it. Neither individuals nor classes reproduce accidently; it is an intentional, purposeful exercise. If individuals or classes unintentionally ignore reproducing, then they intentionally do not plan to reproduce.

One does not fall into success; one must climb up to success.

We do not reproduce because we have no shared expectations.

Expectations are a powerful influence. The great car manufacturer Henry Ford was asked to donate for the construction of a new medical facility. The wealthy industrialist pledged $5,000. The next day the newspaper headlines read, "Henry Ford Contributes $50,000 to the Local Hospital." The irate Ford was on the phone immediately to complain, stating he had been misunderstood. The fund-raiser said that he would reprint a retraction in the following day's paper to read, "Henry Ford reduces his donation by $45,000." Realizing the poor publicity that would result, Mr. Ford agreed to the $50,000 contribution.

We all know the power of expectations. As children we experienced the effect upon us as our parents laid down what they expected. As students, our teachers exercised the power of expectations as revealed by a report card. Employees certainly understand the power of their boss's expectations. Married people know what their spouse expects.

Expectations are the things we presume should be done, and that is why we expect them. They are part of everyone's life and should extend to the Sunday School ministry as well. How can we have a Sunday School in HD if people do not know the expectations of Sunday School? Without expectations all we can expect to see is a fuzzy picture of Sunday School. The Sunday School leader should constantly communicate the expectation of reproducing more leaders.

We do not reproduce when we do not believe the best in people.

Unless proven otherwise, always give people the benefit of the doubt. If you are ever to be used as a reproducer, you must believe the best in people. People are the Sunday School's greatest asset. Given the choice of great facilities, great budget, great resources, or great people, I will take great people every time. If you had all the facilities, budget, and resources you wanted but did not have the people, then your assets would amount to nothing. The best way to change a person is to change how you think and act toward him. If you will treat him according to his potential, then you have a greater chance of drawing that potential out of him and seeing him become what he ought to be.

How Do You Reproduce Others?

It has often been said that you can only reproduce what you are. That is, you "cannot reproduce what you are not." Therefore, the first step in reproducing others is to be somebody! It is imperative that we continue to grow so that we are better equipped to lead others. We can continue to grow by reading good books, interacting with those that can speak into our lives and stretch us, and attending conferences.

Reproduction is a process, not an event. Events should be employed as part of the process, but an event alone will fall short. We have leaned too heavily on an event to accomplish the task for us. Events should be part of the developmental strategy, but they cannot replace the ongoing relationship of a discipler. A mentor must commit to be process driven and not event driven. This once again points to the importance of cyclical Sunday School leadership meetings.

At some point the reproducing process requires the mentee to practice his skill. If you are going to reproduce, then you must use people where they are usable. You cannot involve them in a capacity for which they are not ready. It is imperative that you start where they are. Serving in their current capacity will be a catalyst to greater areas. Small steps lead to greater steps. It is much like teaching a child to ride a bicycle. You start them out with training wheels and gradually build from there. Adult Sunday School teachers should be encouraged to have a member of their class teach once a month. They may not be ready to teach a class full-time, but this gives them the opportunity to practice, learn, and refine their skill so that one day they will be ready. Scripture teaches us that we will reap what we sow. Therefore, if you need ten new teachers next year, you better start sowing now.

Reproducing is more about attitude than ability. It can be rightly argued that ability is part of anyone delivering the goods. I am not discounting the valuable role of ability, but I am saying that reproducing *is more* about attitude than ability. Therefore, a reproducer must have the right attitude, and the one in the process of being produced must have the right attitude.

Reproducing is more about attitude than ability.

Reproducing others is often as simple as being there for them. Developing others is not so much a classroom issue as a life issue. Being a coach and mentor to someone can take that person a long way down the journey. The Bible is full of these types of relationships; consider Moses and Joshua, Eli and Samuel, Elijah and Elisha, Jesus and His disciples, Peter and Mark, Paul and Timothy. When a mentee observes a mentor, he is looking at leadership in HD.

Reproducers need more elimination in their lives to have more concentration. Life throws much at us. We have so many things seeking our involvement. If we are to be used as a reproducer of reproducers, then we must eliminate some stuff from our lives. Any person or organization that excelled was extremely focused.

What Benefits Do the Mentor and Mentee Enjoy Together?

Fulfillment

If you have ever poured your life into others and watched them grow and reach their potential in Christ, then you know the satisfaction that comes from such an endeavor. On the other hand, if you have received mentoring and it has developed you to the point that you are being used of God, then you too have experienced much fulfillment.

Strength

Two are better than one. Therefore, when you mentor someone and he gets involved in the ministry, you have someone else in the battle with you. It was not accidental that Jesus sent His disciples out in teams of two. There is strength in numbers. When you reproduce yourself, you add others to the ministry and have thus strengthened the ministry.

Joy

Joy is greatly enhanced when you share it with others. For the most part, team sports garner more enthusiasm than individual sports. Why? There are more people involved and more folks that enjoy the victory together.

Love

Love must find a way to bestow itself on someone. Love is not satisfied to remain alone. When you help others become what God wants them to be, you form a loving relationship. Likewise, if you were the recipient of a spiritual coach, you have a great love for him.

Deep, Lasting Relationship

I am always amazed at the relationship that is established by soldiers who have fought together. They may go years without seeing each other, but when they do, it is evident that there is a deep and abiding respect and relationship between them. Like soldiers, when you have been in the spiritual foxhole with another soldier of Christ, there is a respect and relationship that exceeds definition.

What Benefits Does the Reproducing Sunday School Enjoy?

It develops people for God's glory.

It is always uplifting to see people develop and bring glory to God.

It builds future leaders.

Tomorrow is coming, and we must continually develop more teachers, outreach leaders, care-group leaders, etc., to meet the needs that tomorrow will bring. The work of God must be carried to the next generation, and only this generation can accomplish that.

It edifies the church.

The amount of people ministered to is in direct proportion to the number of people serving. As more ministry leaders are activated, we can continue to touch more lives with the Word of God and by the people of God.

It greatly multiplies your ministry.

Everyone has some limitations. When you reach your limit, you can only expand your ministry by multiplying yourself through others. By franchising your leadership in others, your influence continues to spread because it will go places that you cannot!

What Are the Results of a Reproducing Sunday School?

Growth is the result of a reproducing Sunday School. Your Sunday School will expand as your leadership base expands. You grow your Sunday School as you grow leaders. Growth is dependent on the widening of the leadership base because the current base can only produce X amount of work.

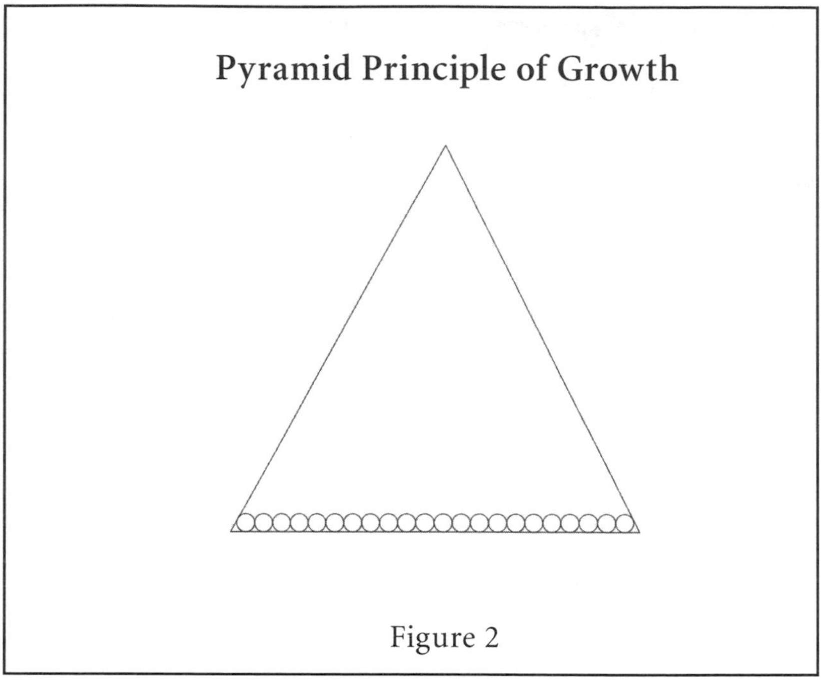

Figure 2

The pyramid in figure 2 represents Sunday School. The base of the pyramid represents teachers as illustrated by the circles along it. The peak of the pyramid represents attendance. Attendance is accumulated by the amount of followers that are stacked on each teacher. Each teacher does not have the same amount of followers because we all have different gifts and abilities. In figure 3 the circles in the middle of the base represent teachers who would have more stacked on them than those toward each end of the base.

The height of the pyramid is directly affected by the width of its base. That is, if you want the peak of the pyramid higher, then you must widen the base. This perfectly illustrates Sunday School growth. If you want to increase your Sunday School attendance, then you must reproduce more teachers as illustrated in figure 4.

Pyramid Principle of Growth

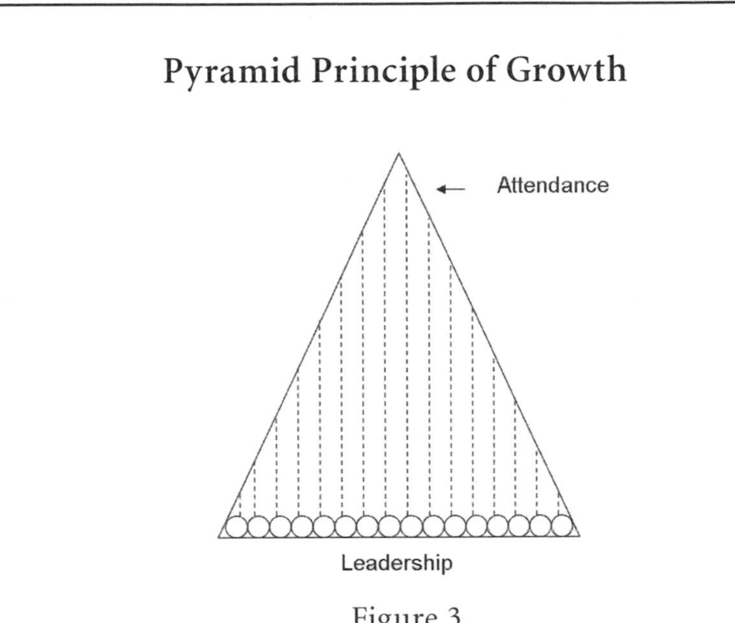

Figure 3

Pyramid Principle of Growth

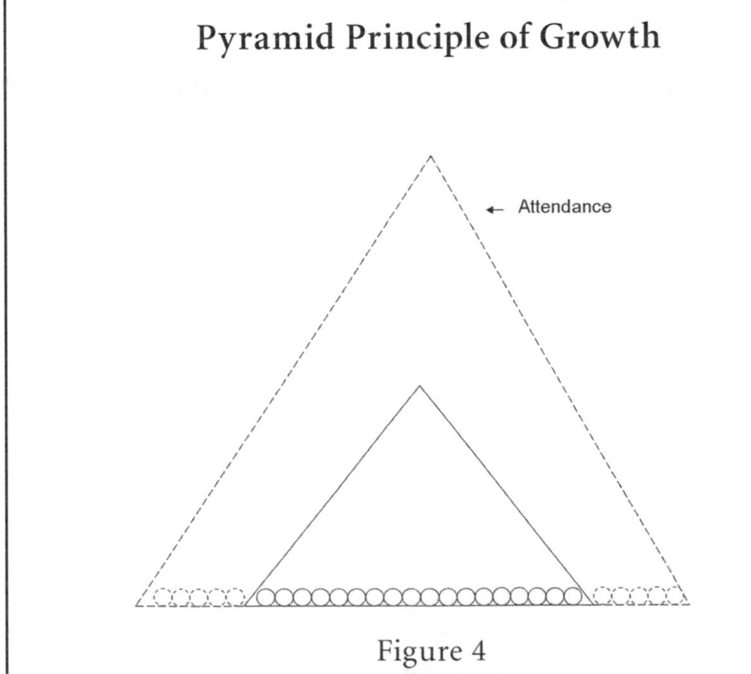

Figure 4

The base of the pyramid is the cause that produces the effect that we refer to as attendance. Sunday Schools are not growing due to a lack of concern over attendance. If our concern for greater attendance equated to a greater audience, we would be in good shape. Our challenge is that we must be concerned with producing more leaders and expanding the leadership base as we should. We need to concern ourselves more with the cause that produces the effect.

In Exodus 18 Moses was a do-it-all-yourself leader until Jethro provided him some great leadership advice. Like Moses, some leaders choose to put it all on their own shoulders and not reproduce themselves in others as Paul instructed young Timothy.

> "And the things that you have heard from me among many witnesses, commit these to faithful men who will be able to teach others also." (2 Tim. 2:2)

This method of leadership inverts the growth pyramid as seen in figure 5.

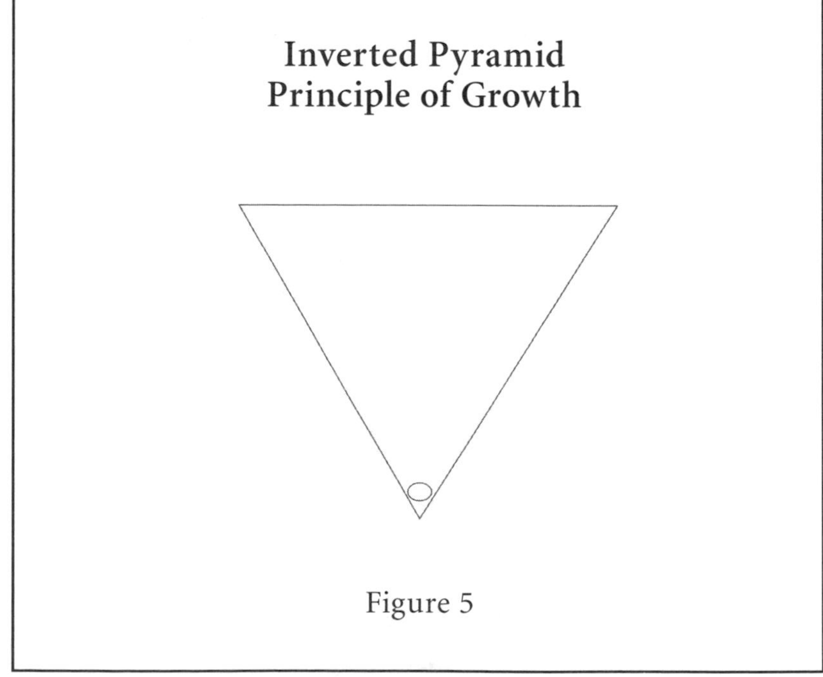

Figure 5

I have a relationship with a church that researched the last ten years of their ministry and gave me a copy of their findings. I was particularly interested in the section on their Sunday School. I was struck with sadness when I read that their average Sunday School attendance increased by only one person in ten years. As I continued reading, I saw that their current number of Sunday School classes was exactly the same as it was a decade earlier. The tragedy of this church was the leadership base stayed static for ten solid years! The tragedy was not that their attendance was stationary but that the cause never prompted an effect. By not developing new teachers and widening the leadership base of their Sunday School, this church practiced birth control. They birthed no new leaders and, consequently, no new classes so they experienced no new growth. This was not their intention, but without the intentionality of reproducing, this Sunday School went childless.

Every Sunday School needs intentionally to pursue more teachers. To be unintentional in developing more teachers is intentionally to stagnate your Sunday School. The formula is simple: more teachers = more classes = more workers = more ministry. Where do we start with this newfound intentionally? We begin in the adult division of the Sunday School. Classes in every age division must have adult leaders to survive, and adult leaders are found in adult classes. At this point I want to make a big statement. The adult division of the Sunday School is the most strategic area of ministry in the church! I did not say that it was more important than these other ministries; I said it was more strategic. Not only is the adult division of the Sunday School strategic for the younger age divisions of the Sunday School, but it is also strategic in producing leaders for other ministries throughout the church.

The adult division of the Sunday School is the most strategic area of ministry in the church!

I want to make another big statement. *If your adult teachers do not embrace this concept, they will stalemate your church!* They must see this concept with the clarity of high definition. Our churches depend on it.

The essence of leadership is not gathering a crowd of followers but reproducing more leaders. Having followers is undoubtedly part of leadership, but it does not embody the ultimate leadership ambition. The following two categories represent leaders. The goal is to grow from a leader with followers to a leader who reproduces more leaders.

A Leader Who Has Followers	**Versus**	**A Leader Who Reproduces Leaders**
Shows some leadership		Shows significant leadership
Has shallow leadership		Has deep leadership
Is a good leader		Is a great leader
Has little influence		Has much influence
Is a micro leader		Is a macro leader
Is narrow in thinking		Is broad in thinking
Is concerned with self		Is concerned with the organization
Is insecure		Is secure
Is ego-driven		Is cause-driven
Maximizes some potential		Maximizes great potential
Believes in himself		Believes in others
Produces some growth		Produces much growth
Has a fruitful ministry		Has a franchising ministry
Occupies territory		Takes new territory
See growth by addition		Sees growth by multiplication
Grows his class		Grows the organization
Focuses on his kingdom		Focuses on God's kingdom

The first category represents people that are good folks and have some leadership capabilities. They are helping the church, but they may not be maximizing their God-given potential and influence to expand the church and her ministry. They may be growing their class, but they are not extending the leadership base of the Sunday School pyramid.

If there is an entity in the church that can reproduce more servants and more leaders, it is the Sunday School.

This principle of reproduction not only applies to the Sunday School organization, but it also pertains to the church as a whole and to individual classes. The more people who are involved in the leadership base of the church pyramid, the more ministry is accomplished by the church. Likewise, the more people who are involved in the leadership base of the class pyramid, the more ministry is accomplished by the class. Some churches have inverted the pyramid to the point that her ministry rides completely on the shoulders of the pastor. Again, the analogy applies to the class where everything is dependent on the teacher. This scenario, illustrated in figure 4 on page 111, produces no growth and much burnout.

If there is an entity in the church that can reproduce more servants and more leaders, it is the Sunday School. As I said to open this chapter, the greatest thing a Sunday School can do to infuse energy and vitality into her organization is to see lives changed and people saved. The second greatest thing it can do to inject life into the Sunday School ministry is to reproduce new leaders!

CHAPTER 8

Growth Factors

Growth, ah, the thing we all strive for, labor for, and exert blood, sweat, and tears for! Like hunters, we are always on the chase for it; like lions, we are always on the prowl for it; like fishermen, we are always throwing new bait at it. Growth is the thing for which we pull out our hair, trying desperately to get our arms around it. We suffer much anguish as we struggle to get a mental and philosophical grip of it. The pursuit of growth brings passion and persecution, thrills and tribulations, invigoration and indigestion. It is like fishing for a big bass only to come up with a tiny blue gill! Growth is such a valued commodity, yet it often eludes us.

Church growth is not as simple as it seems. It is complex and has many components. It seems the older I get, the less I know about the subject. The one thing we do know about growth is that God wants it, the world needs it, the church should experience it, and we can never be negotiable with it! To negotiate growth is to negotiate souls. We have no right to tolerate any barrier that limits church growth. Why? The church is not ours; she belongs to God who purchased her with the blood of His Son. Only God has the right to negotiate growth. My dear friend and staff colleague, Dan Dorner, says, “We must remove every man-made impediment that hinders church growth.” I could not agree more!

There are many factors that contribute to church growth. Sunday School growth is a large contributor in this church growth mix. Any church attempting to grow while ignoring their Sunday School will experience an exercise in futility. Obviously, growth is predominantly directed by spiritual issues like the hand of God on the church, prayer, etc. The purpose of this chapter is to consider the practical hands-on issues that surround growth. The following nine factors work collectively and interactively in the growth mix. They affect not only overall church growth but also Sunday School growth.

The one thing we do know about growth is that God wants it, the world needs it, the church should experience it, and we can never be negotiable with it!

Growth Factors

Attitude is paramount.

It may not be well received to spend money and time to travel to another city for a church growth conference only to hear someone lecture the entire time on attitude. However, it might be the best thing any of us could do to help facilitate growth in our congregation. Attitude is the key to growth. Two people join the church on the same day, yet five years later one is a growing, maturing, committed Christian while the other is still a babe in Christ who has seen no growth toward spiritual maturity. Why is one developing and growing and the other is not? It is not personality; it is not IQ; it is not charisma, etc. It is attitude! One has a growth attitude while the other does not.

If you are a believer, the most important thing inside you is the Holy Spirit; the second most important thing in you is your attitude! Your attitude is something you get to choose because it is not ability; it is a choice.

> Let this mind be in you which was also in Christ Jesus. (Phil. 2:5)

Skills, intelligence, charisma, and personality are wonderful to have, but they cannot unseat attitude in importance. The world is full of talented, gifted, smart people who accomplish little. Ability alone will not get the job done. Cemeteries are full of those who died having never accomplished much or having never tapped into all of their God-given potential because of their attitude! Therefore, we need a better "Attitude Quotient" than we do an "Intelligence Quotient." Ability defines your potential; attitude determines if you reach it.

> For as he thinks within himself, so he is." (Prov. 23:7 HCSB)

You become what you think. So *how* you think is important. You get to choose how you think! Sunday School leaders must always be working on the attitudes of others. We must always remind ourselves that growth is an attitude and we should attend to it.

Under the inspiration of the Holy Spirit, the great apostle Paul said that the three greatest things were "faith, hope, and love" (1 Cor. 13:13). I submit to you that these three things are attitudes, not abilities. You do not acquire faith through your skill set; you acquire it through your attitude. You do not have hope because you are talented; you have hope because of your attitude. You do not love because you are gifted; you love because of your attitude. Did I say that your "AQ" is more important than your IQ? The greatest thing a Sunday School leader can do is to help people love God and be obedient to Him. The next best thing is to help them have the right attitude.

Here is my theory for church growth. Small churches need to think like big churches. They need to operate like big churches and embrace attitudes that helped them grow. Big churches need to think like small churches. They should have the attitude that our church is a close-knit family. Big churches should have the attitude that everyone matters and everyone wants to be known and loved. Both lines of thinking deal with attitude.

It is imperative that we understand that growth is an attitude, not a method, skill, or technique. If a church has the attitude to grow, they will. Conversely, if they do not have an attitude to grow, they will not. We should always be evaluating and working on our attitudes.

Control freaks paralyze ministry.

This issue is really an attitude issue as well, but I thought it best to deal with it separately. If someone is controlling everything, then the only thing that can get done is what he does. The principle applies if it is a few people controlling everything. They still limit the church by their own limitations. Some churches have two or three patriarchs or matriarchs that control everything in the church. I just recently had a pastor sit in my office for two hours distraught and crying because his church was struggling to loose herself from the stronghold of three power brokers in his church. They were constantly running off pastors, and he was currently in the crosshairs of their scope. Yet the church was growing under his leadership. People were being saved and baptized, and others were joining the church. One would think that everyone would rejoice over that, but a problem occurs for church power brokers when the church is expanding. They lose control. This church that was neat, tidy, and just the way they wanted it was now becoming something they could not control. The larger an organization grows, the smaller an individual's piece of pie becomes.

Patriarch and matriarch churches stop growing by design. Those in charge will not lose control. Therefore, they place a lid on the church and her ability to grow. Sunday School classes and departments have these same patriarch and matriarch issues. It was the same problem that the elder brother in Luke 15 had with his younger, prodigal brother coming back home. The elder brother had the farm, his father, and the servants all to himself. The last thing he wanted was for baby brother to come home and mess everything up that he had going. I call classes that fit this description "Elder Brother Sunday School Classes."

John Maxwell was right when he said, "You must give up to go up." I have personally experienced this as our church has grown. There have been some ministries that I love doing that I have had to relinquish or else I would stymie growth. Remember that growth is never negotiable! Sometimes the best we can do to continue growth is to get out of the way.

The opposite of control is empowerment. Sunday School leaders need to heed the five *E*s.

- Enlist
- Equip
- Empower
- Encourage
- Evaluate

We should not be guilty of having gifted, committed people sit around doing nothing because we are afraid to turn ministry over to someone else. The apostle Paul started churches, developed godly leaders, and turned them loose by empowering them with the ministry.

Quit chasing problems and start seizing opportunities!

Most of our leadership energy is spent solving problems when it should be invested in seizing our opportunities. Churches are full of problems because churches are full of people. I think we can all agree that we will never solve all our problems; that is impossible. As long as we are in this sin-cursed world, we will have problems. Since Adam and Eve's fall in the garden of Eden, the world has been overrun with problems.

Now, certainly there are problems that need to be addressed and solved. Use wisdom here. The issue is to know which problems to tackle and which problems to live with. However, do not get so hung up with your problems that you can never pursue opportunities!

You can *spend* time and energy, or you can *invest* time and energy. If all you do is solve problems, then you are *spending* your time and energy. If you are pursuing your dream, vision, and opportunities, then you are *investing* your time and energies. You will never grow a ministry by solving all your problems.

A young lady served an internship with us. She had a passion for Sunday School and soaked up everything she could during her short tenure. Before leaving she sat down with me to discuss a dilemma that she would walk into when she went to her church. She knew she had three teachers who would not get on board with her. So she asked, "What am I going to do about that?" I replied, "Nothing. You can't solve all your problems. So why would you go pour your time and energy into three teachers that won't grow with you? Pour your time and energy into the other twenty-two teachers that will grow with you. You won't produce growth from every class, so pursue your growth opportunities, not your problems." My rule of thumb is for leaders to stop pouring 80 percent of their time and energy into their problems and start putting 80 percent of their time and energy into their opportunities. Time and energy are limited resources, so use them wisely.

Sunday morning rules.

Adhere to this principle if you want to grow. Notice I did not say that Sunday night rules, or Wednesday night rules, or the church basketball league rules, or the church child care center rules. I said that Sunday morning rules, and this should have far-reaching ramifications throughout the church. This means every aspect of church life should reflect this growth principle.

- The budget should be constructed with a priority on Sunday morning.
- Staff should be hired with Sunday morning in mind.
- Facilities should be built and prioritized based on Sunday morning ministries.
- Equipment and resources should be purchased and allocated around Sunday morning.

You see, Sunday morning rules! Why? You cannot grow a church without a quality Sunday morning. You can have the greatest Sunday night, Wednesday night, basketball league, and child care center there is and still not grow a church if Sunday morning is not kicking. Conversely, if Sunday morning is zinging, then you can grow even if these other events are sub-par. Sunday morning rules!

I am not opposed to the other activities I mentioned. They have their place and add some value to a church and her ministries, but I have also seen them become the "tail that wags the dog" in the allocation of church energies, resources, and emphases. This is damaging to the overall purpose of the church. It is evident that before a church can be anything else, she must first be the church! And the church is never more the church than when she meets on Sunday mornings.

It is evident that before a church can be anything else, she must first be the church!

Quality is essential in five key areas on Sunday morning.

- Parking
- Preaching
- Music
- Sunday School
- Hospitality

All five of these key Sunday morning ingredients greatly affect one another. If a church has great preaching and terrible music, it will adversely affect the worship service attendance. If the church has a great Sunday School class for a visiting couple to attend but no one to show them how to get to the room, then she has shot herself in the foot. A church is wise to evaluate these five components and to give the greatest priority to the one that is most lacking because it can render the other four ineffective.

Resources require a balancing act.

You must balance four things to keep growth at its maximum:

- Parking Space
- Worship Space
- Educational Space
- Budget

Parking is often overlooked in the growth equation. People come to church in cars, not by foot, so the church must make appropriate accommodations. My twin brother, Arden, is a pastor, and he and I have worked together consulting with some churches. We consulted with one church that would see their attendance hit five hundred from time to time but could never go above that or sustain that mark. The first thing we did when we visited the church was to count parking spaces; they had 143 parking spaces. Most churches average about two people per car, which means their church could park 286 people. We could not believe they were actually running up to five hundred. Upon our interviews with them, the obvious was revealed. They had people parking in the grass, out on the street, and anywhere else they could find. Next we measured every pew to see how many bodies would comfortably fit into the worship center. They thought the worship center would hold around six hundred. This was determined based on each person getting an eighteen-inch space. Most people do not fit comfortably into an eighteen-inch seat. They had them crammed in there like a can of sardines! We made two simple recommendations: add parking, and go to two worship services. After this was achieved their attendance shot up by 37 percent in three months. This church did not have a spiritual problem; they had a logistics problem.

In his book *Natural Church Development*, Christian Swartz used the illustration that a barrel could only hold as much water as the lowest slat allowed. This is a great illustration depicting the balance that is needed between the four resources mentioned above. You may be able to park one thousand people, but if your worship center can only seat five hundred then it's a low slat in the barrel. You must lengthen the worship center slat by increasing its size or have two morning worship services. To do nothing with this slat is to negotiate growth, and growth is never negotiable! So shore up the low slat.

As you consider your growth potential, you must always evaluate the balance of parking space, worship space, and education space. I recognize that money underwrites all three spaces, but church leaders should know the facts regarding each space area and take measures to lengthen the lowest slat whether that is additional facilities or multiple usage of your current space.

Growth necessitates simplicity and focus.

Leaders should keep things simple and maintain focus. Church should not be complicated. Most every mainline denomination would agree that the five purposes of a New Testament are found in the book of Acts—worship, evangelism, discipleship, ministry, and fellowship. These five functions are not complicated or controversial; they are simple and obvious. It is a natural tendency for organizations with a long tenure to get offtrack. The mission that originated the organization seems to lose footing over time as new people and new cultures emerge. Church is no different; Sunday School is no different. Leaders must first know what the main thing is. Second, they must keep the main thing as the main thing.

Stories abound of churches that started out well, grew, and saw many conversions only to start drifting away from the Great Commission. What was once a great church is now a mediocre church or even a struggling church. I have seen Sunday Schools do the same. I was once asked what my greatest challenge was personally and what my greatest challenge was as a minister of education. I responded by stating the challenge is the same for both—focus! I must personally stay focused, and I must continually keep our Sunday School focused. It is so easy to get offtrack. So, when it comes to focus, leaders must be tenacious.

I have a theory that goes like this: little things in the church become big when big things in the church first become little. How do big things get little? The same way little things get big—by losing focus! The old proverbial story of the church splitting over the color of the carpet applies here. Why would a church split over the color of the carpet? Does it really matter? Does God care what color the carpet is? After all, He made all the colors, so I assume God likes them all. So why is there so much fuss? I will tell you why: because the church allowed the big thing—the Great Commission—to become a little thing first. You show me a church that is on fire for souls and serious about discipling people in the Word of God, and I will show you a church that will never split over an incidental like the color of the carpet! When the big thing is in its proper place, there is no room available for little things to wiggle their way in. Just as soon as the big thing slips away from its rightful place, then little things have opportunity to occupy their place. Mark it down that when nonessentials become essential, it was first preceded by the essentials becoming nonessential! Church leaders must maintain focus at all time!

When it comes to focus, leaders must be tenacious.

The Preschool Ministry must continually be emphasized!

This is the most difficult ministry in the church to man. Everyone needs to know this, and everyone needs to work toward meeting this need! I have often said that preschool teachers will receive the greatest rewards in heaven because they are not serving to receive accolades from man. Churches try many things to get more people involved in this important ministry. Often these efforts fall short of our desires, but at least they keep the significance before the people. You will not have all the answers, but everyone should do all they can to lend help and support the preschool ministry. Be liberal in your support and emphasis of the preschool ministry. This department should get the best facility and resources in the church, which is an enormous way to support this vital ministry and give credence to it. These resources will be most valuable as they help keep good morale with preschool teachers.

In order to experience ongoing growth, you must continually pull the next generation into the church. Young people are more "marketable" for the church. The older you are, the more settled you become. Age tends to lessen change and establish people in a community and in a church if they choose to attend a church. Young people experience much change as they go from college to starting their careers and families. As a result, they become more "marketable" to the church. That being the case, a church will not reach young families with inferior preschool facilities. Young parents will not put their child into a facility unless it is as clean, nice, and safe as their environment at home.

I have a pet peeve: do not call the preschool ministry the "nursery." "Nursery" communicates that it is a ministry that just wipes noses and bottoms. It is a teaching ministry that sees to the youngest and most vulnerable in the church. The greatest years of learning occur between birth and five years of age. Therefore, we should have teachers, not just caretakers, serving in preschool classes.

Victories should be celebrated without creating sacred cows.

People do not join organizations because of where they have been. Rather, they join because of where they are headed. The best way to ruin your future is continually to rehearse your past. A team does not win the championship by sitting around rehearsing last year's successes, and neither does a church. It is so natural to relish in those great victories of yesteryear. Understand that success is wonderful, but success breeds sacred cows. No victories, no sacred cows. Obviously, a church needs to celebrate her victories. You work hard for them, and they should be enjoyed for a season. Afterward, it is time to move on. Be careful that you do not overly cling to that which was once beneficial but has since lost its effectiveness.

People do not join your church to perpetuate your glorious past. New and potential members have no point of reference to the past. They join with a vision to forge the future. This is true of churches, and it is true of Sunday School classes.

Facilities make a statement.

Facilities should have good curb appeal. The care of church facilities makes a huge statement to visitors and potential new members. The community should not see the church building as the "neighborhood eyesore." Even unchurched neighbors should value the church building as attractive to the community. The church facility gives credence to the old adage, "You never have a second chance to make a first impression."

> **The best way to ruin your future is continually to rehearse your past.**

Facilities should look like someone cares. Facilities should also look like we are expecting company. Every family has experienced an unexpected visit to their home. Once you discover that your unanticipated company will soon arrive, you scurry around picking up the place. Why? Company is coming. Too many churches and too many Sunday School rooms look as if company will never darken the door. Many Sunday School rooms have an old dusty piano in the corner with hymnbooks and quarterlies stacked on top. They have a basket made from Popsicle sticks at Vacation Bible School to collect offering envelopes. Multiple usages of rooms multiply the problem. Because the room must be used for other activities during the week, each program gets to deposit their fair share of junk. Take a walk around your facilities occasionally and look with a critiquing eye. Look at your facilities through the eyes of a visitor.

Facilities should have proper signage. This includes outside signage as well as inside signage. When visitors drive on campus, they need to know where to park and where to get information and directions. These little things help the visitor have a good experience and want to return. When visitors see the effort exerted to make their experiences positive, they sense they are both welcomed and wanted.

Proper room identification is imperative. Churches are guilty of calling a room what it used to be instead of what it is. For example "the old church parlor" or "the old choir room" would be unfamiliar to many people. New people have no point of reference to the past, so call the room what it currently is. Rooms are sometimes called by the name of the class that meets in it, such as "the Dorcas Class," "the Promise Class," "the Men's Class," or "the Singles Class." Visitors do not know rooms by the name of the class; they know rooms based on a proper numbering system.

Facilities should also look like we are expecting company.

Finally, your facilities should be suitably situated on your campus. Ask some pertinent questions about your building. Why will you place the worship center at this particular place on the church property? Where should the various age division departments be located? The outlay of your buildings is critical and so is the positioning of your age divisions. Often it is difficult to adequately position every building and every age division within the buildings. Lay of the land, topography, sequence of land purchases, and budget contribute to this challenge. I recommend the following diagram as a blueprint.

Facility Layout

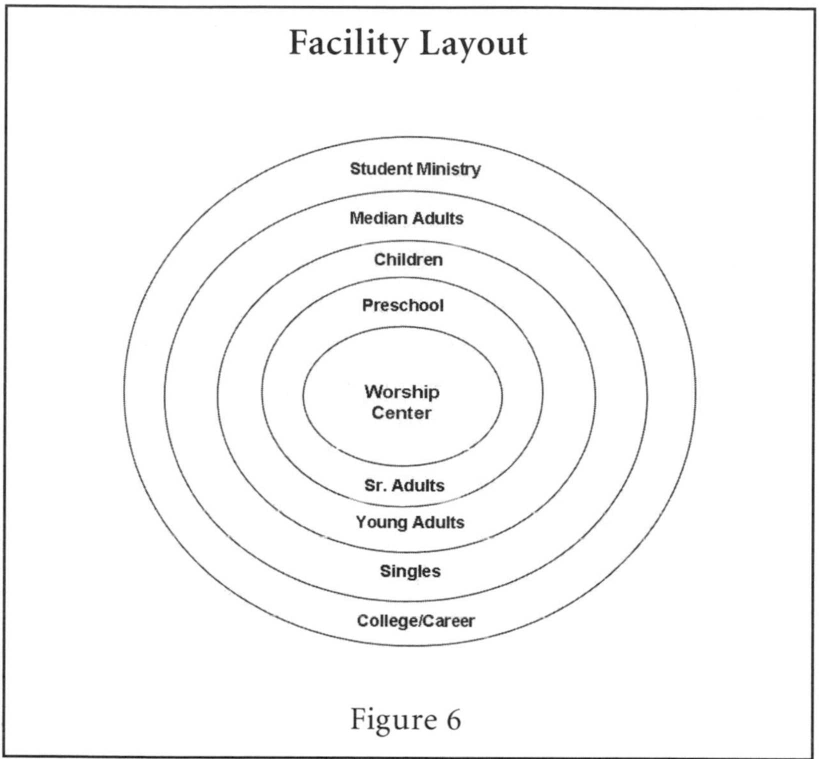

Figure 6

The inner circle is the worship center. Ideally, it would be situated in the center of your property with equal amounts of other facilities and equal amounts of parking around it. Notice the distribution of age divisions in proximity to the worship center as represented by the concentric circles.

The second circle represents the preschool and senior adult departments. The youngest and the oldest cannot get around like everyone else. Therefore, they should have the space closest to the worship center.

The third circle signifies the children's and young adult departments. Children should not have to travel far, and young adults want to be close to their preschoolers.

The fourth circle is for the median adults and singles. Median adults would have some elementary children and would want to be as close to them as possible. Also, many singles have children so they need to be given this same consideration.

The last circle represents the youth and college departments. They are on their first set of legs so distance is not a factor. In addition, they make a lot of noise so, well, you know.

The church choir sings with a mixture of notes that complement one another producing a harmonious sound which we enjoy. Each pitch is combined with the others in such a way as to enhance them. These nine growth factors are to work with one another in like manner. One can hurt the others or augment them. This is not an exhaustive list of issues affecting church growth. However, these nine are critical for the church leader who wants to take new territory.

THE LEADERSHIP OF SUNDAY SCHOOL IN HD

---

leadership: capacity or ability to lead (*Webster's II New College Dictionary*)

CHAPTER 9

The Essentials of Leadership

What keeps a Sunday School ministry from being a "Sunday School in HD"? They do not have a "Sunday School leader in HD." The number one cause that determines whether you have a well-defined Sunday School is leadership. It is impossible to grow a great Sunday School ministry with a weak leader. In his book *Good to Great*, Jim Collins was right when he said you must get the right people in the right seats on the bus.

It is true that . . .

- If you want to know the temperature of the church, stick the thermometer in the preacher's mouth.
- If you want to know the temperature of a home, stick the thermometer in the parent's mouth.
- If you want to know the temperature of the business, stick the thermometer in the CEO's mouth.
- If you want to know the temperature of the team, stick the thermometer in the coach's mouth.
- If you want to know the temperature of the class, stick the thermometer in the teacher's mouth.
- If you want to know the temperature of the Sunday School, stick the thermometer in the Sunday School leader's mouth!

You see, having a Sunday School in HD starts with leadership. May I emphatically say to you that no other variables affect your Sunday School like her leadership! A church must use great wisdom and exercise great diligence in selecting Sunday School leadership.

The Church's Two Key Sunday School Leaders

The first key leader of the Sunday School ministry is the *pastor*. The pastor's role of leadership in Sunday School cannot be overstated. It has been my observation that Sunday Schools rise and fall with the pastor's perspective of the work of Sunday School within the context of the local church. Some pastors understand the vital role Sunday School plays in the church while others do not. There are two key functions of the pastor's leadership in Sunday School.

The first function of the pastor's Sunday School leadership is being a *champion*. That is, the pastor must champion the cause of Sunday School. To do this, he must understand the role Sunday School plays in his church. The pastor cannot practically be hands-on with everything that goes on in Sunday School such as ordering literature, setting up rooms, enlisting all the workers, etc. However, he must champion the cause of Sunday School. It has been my observation that Sunday Schools grow when the pastor campaigns for Sunday School because what is important to the leader becomes important to the people.

The pastor must champion the cause of Sunday School.

How can the pastor champion the cause of Sunday School? I think it starts by his joining and attending a Sunday School class himself. His example will send an unequivocal message to the entire congregation that Sunday School is important around here! Some pastors do not have this option because of worship services and Sunday School taking place simultaneously, but if the option is available, the wise pastor will lead by example. Furthermore, the pastor can champion the cause of Sunday School by speaking about it when he is before the people on Sunday mornings. Whether through announcements or incorporated into his sermons, the people need to hear their pastor talk about Sunday School. Again, what is important to the pastor becomes important to the people. Lastly, the pastor can champion the cause of Sunday School by making sure the budget supports Sunday School. I say this knowing that all pastors and all churches have financial limitations. I do not know any church that has all the resources it needs. My point is that pastors should strive to provide the basic resources needed to place their Sunday School in an environment conducive for growth. It is obvious that Sunday School needs a certain amount of facilities and curriculum. There is one aspect of a budget that is often overlooked—training dollars. There is a direct relationship between training and growth. If you want a growing Sunday School, then you must have trained, equipped, competent workers. It is a colossal mistake to ignore the training of your workers and not to underwrite this in your annual budget because they are the greatest asset a Sunday School ministry has. These are not dollars that are spent; they are dollars invested. These dollars will come back to you when your staff becomes skilled and qualified.

The second function of the pastor's Sunday School leadership is being a *cheerleader*. No one can encourage the people like their pastor because people love to please their pastor. When the pastor recognizes Sunday School workers for their good work, he is pouring fuel on an already burning fire. I have watched my pastor, Dr. Johnny Hunt, do this time and again. His encouragement has infused our Sunday School with more morale than any other single factor. He fires them up, and the heat of that fire radiates throughout our classes. I have observed many pastors who have lifted their Sunday Schools to another level by championing the cause of Sunday School and cheering on their Sunday School workers. Come on, pastor, help us out. When you do, your people will love you for it!

The second critical leader of the Sunday School is the *minister of education* or *Sunday School director.* This person will have more direct and more frequent contact with the soldiers in the field. A minority of churches have a paid staff person overseeing the Sunday School ministry. Since the average church runs ninety-three in Sunday School attendance, most have a volunteer layperson as their Sunday School director. The issue is not whether the person is on staff or not but *who* the person is! So I will refer to the minister of education or the Sunday School director as the *Sunday School leader.*

No one can encourage the people like their pastor because people love to please their pastor.

Too many Sunday School leaders are nothing more than glorified secretaries. That is, they order the curriculum, collect the class rolls each week, and tally the total attendance. This is not leadership; this is secretarial work. Secretaries are needed to keep things organized, on time, and running smoothly. However, the Sunday School leader is not supposed to be the Sunday School secretary, and too many have never made that distinction.

Many churches use a nominating committee to enlist workers on an annual basis at the start of the new church year. You set yourself up for a fall if you use a nominating committee to select your Sunday School leaders. By design the nominating committee is postured for failure because it is not possible for a group of six people to know about all the positions of service in the church and then have time to properly enlist all the workers for those positions. Consequently, they become a committee of slot fillers. They have *X* amount of slots to fill, so they do just that: they fill slots. I have seen some negative things come out of this practice.

If a nominating committee is not used, then who should enlist the workers for the various ministries? The person leading each ministry should shoulder this responsibility. For example, the Sunday School leader should enlist Sunday School teachers and workers because this will be the team with which he must work. This should be true for every ministry in the church. The principle is simple; if you have no input into your personnel, you are not the team leader. This practice is evident in other organizations. Every CEO hires his own staff, and every coach selects his own assistants. Sunday School workers cannot share the Sunday School leader's vision and direction for the ministry if they are not enlisted by him. Thus, we have constructed a ministry team that is already positioned for problems.

The selection of the church's Sunday School leader should be done by the pastor or his designate as should every other ministry leader in the church. The same rationale applies that every leader should be enlisted by the person to whom he will answer. Every leader has the right to enlist those who will commit to his vision, especially the pastor. The Sunday School leader must serve in submission to and coordination with his pastor. The Sunday School ministry is too large to be a Lone Ranger ministry that is not in sync with the pastor.

Leaders Set Three Key Things in Place

If you want to have a great Sunday School ministry, then it is imperative that you have a great Sunday School workforce! You just cannot throw anyone into a spiritual leadership position. We are guilty of enlisting about 95 percent of our problems because we do not *enlist;* we fill slots. Each ministry leader should meet leadership standards. Therefore, each ministry must have a process of proper enlistment. This takes time, but not as much time as correcting a situation in which the wrong person is leading! We must

> **We are guilty of enlisting about 95 percent of our problems because we do not *enlist;* we fill slots.**

choose leaders with much thought and prayer. The night before Jesus selected His disciples, He spent the night in prayer.

> Now it came to pass in those days that He went out to the mountain to pray, and continued all night in prayer to God. And when it was day, He called His disciples to Himself; and from them He chose twelve whom He also named apostles." (Luke 6:12–13)

Leaders set many things into place, but there are three things in particular upon which the ministry turns. The leader sets standards, direction, and atmosphere for the ministry, and all three are critical to the well-being of the organization.

Sunday School leaders set *standards*. Jethro taught Moses to choose ministry leaders who met ministry standards. He recommended that potential leaders first be qualified by meeting certain criteria. Only those that met the predetermined values would be given consideration.

> "Moreover you shall select from all the people able men, such as fear God, men of truth, hating covetousness; and place such over them to be rulers of thousands, rulers of hundreds, rulers of fifties, and rulers of tens." . . . And Moses chose able men out of all Israel, and made them heads over the people: rulers of thousands, rulers of hundreds, rulers of fifties, and rulers of tens. (Exod. 18:21, 25)

The standard to be met consisted of these four criteria:

- Men that were capable—"able men"
- Men that feared God—"such as fear God"
- Men that believed and represented the truth—"men of truth"
- Men that disdained covetousness—"hating covetousness"

Moses chose these spiritually competent men; a committee did not choose them ("Moreover *you* shall select"). These men would serve with Moses so it was only proper for Moses to select his team.

The selection of the right people was critical to the success of the ministry. The people needed to be judged appropriately and served by godly leaders. Without standards for the selection process, this could have gone awry. Ministry standards give people comfort in knowing their leaders are qualified to serve in a leadership capacity. This practice is continued in the New Testament. When the apostles needed help in administering the needs of the poor, seven men were chosen who met certain criteria (Acts 6). When Paul instructed Timothy about those who would be bishops, he laid out particular standards they were to meet (1 Tim. 3). James and Matthew indicate that teachers of the Word are held to a higher standard.

> My brethren, let not many of you become teachers, knowing that we shall receive a stricter judgment. (James 3:1)

> "Don't assume that I came to destroy the Law or the Prophets. I did not come to destroy but to fulfill. For I assure you: Until heaven and earth pass away, not the smallest letter or one stroke of a letter will pass from the law until all things are accomplished. Therefore, whoever breaks one of the least of these commandments and teaches people to do so will be called least in the kingdom of heaven. But whoever practices and teaches these commandments will be called great in the kingdom of heaven." (Matt. 5:17–19 HCSB)

The idea of spiritual leaders first being qualified is scattered throughout the Bible. Jesus Himself set forth this principle.

> "For everyone to whom much is given, for him much will be required; and to whom much has been committed, of him they will ask the more." (Luke 12:48)

It is no wonder that both Jeremiah and Malachi rebuked the priests for not living as spiritual leaders should and for not upholding God's Word and their ministry obligations.

Sunday School leaders also *set direction*. They point the ministry in the direction of her journey. Sunday School leaders must understand what Sunday School is about and what she is supposed to do. If the leader does not know this, then the ministry will flounder. I have a six-point strategy for establishing the direction for Sunday School.

1. Conviction

A leader gets conviction from the Word of God. God's Word clearly speaks to the mission of a New Testament church. The Great Commission is our marching orders. Therefore, the leader must possess biblical convictions about the Sunday School. We do not lead by consensus; we lead by conviction. My conviction is that we are to pursue the Great Commission, evangelism, and discipleship, through the Sunday School. I also believe we are to minister to the needs of the people we serve through Sunday School because ministry best takes place in the context of relationships, and relationships best take place within the context of a small group. Therefore, ministry best takes place through Sunday School. At First Baptist Church Woodstock we preach and practice the "three tasks of Sunday School," which are to *reach people*, *teach people*, and *minister to people.*

Conviction always gives direction. Leaders should direct the ministry based on their core convictions. To have no direction is to have no conviction. My biblical conviction as to the three purposes of Sunday School provides my direction. We believe that these three things make up the Sunday School to-do list.

2. Clarity

Now that we have a biblical conviction and direction for our Sunday School, we are to clarify it with the rest of the organization. Biblical convictions are personally beneficial but are organizationally dormant until they are communicated to the organization. Peter taught that spiritual gifts are basically divided into the two categories of speaking gifts and serving gifts.

> As each one has received a gift, minister it to one another, as good stewards of the manifold grace of God. If anyone *speaks*, let him speak as the oracles of God. If anyone *ministers*, let him do it as with the ability which God supplies, that in all things God may be glorified through Jesus Christ, to whom belong the glory and the dominion forever and ever. Amen. (1 Pet. 4:10–11, *emphasis mine*)

Leaders must be speakers because they have to bring clarity to the convictions and direction of the ministry.

3. Consistency

Clarity is strengthened by consistently saying and doing the same things. There needs to be a sense of repetitiveness and predictability from the leader. Behaving consistently and constantly sends the same message out over and over again. Leader, take it as a compliment when someone says, "I knew you were going to say that." Consistency promotes your vision and direction; inconsistency sabotages your vision and direction. Not to continue to communicate the same message is to incapacitate your own leadership.

4. Certainty

When people know that you have set Sunday School on a course drawn from biblical convictions and that you have clarified it and remained consistent with it, then they become certain about it. Uncertain people accomplish little. Coaching high school football taught me that a player would not be aggressive when he was unsure of his assignment. It was my job as coach to make sure my players understood exactly what they were to do on each play. I like to win, and it is impossible to win football games with passive players on the field. When they were absolutely certain what they were to do, they could "lay their ears back" and go for it. I want my Sunday School leaders to "lay their ears back" and go for it. I want them aggressively to pursue the three tasks of Sunday School. Therefore, I constantly remind them of these three tasks.

5. Commitment

Once people become certain, they can now commit. Why did the disciples commit to Jesus? They were so certain that He was the Messiah, the Son of God, that most of them died a martyr's death. Dear friend, you will not die for that which is uncertain. In fact, you will only be faithful and committed to that for which you have no doubts. We often blame people for not being committed when, in fact, the Sunday School leader is yet to have convictions, give clarity, and stay consistent to the point people can be certain about that which they are asked to be committed!

6. Challenge

The final step of the strategy to set your Sunday School's direction is challenge. You see, when all the other steps are in place, your leaders will now be your advocates. They will be out challenging others to get on board as well. Now you have a Sunday School in HD. People clearly see it, get it, and pass it along to others.

The last key thing a Sunday School leader sets in place is *atmosphere*. They get to shape the heart of the ministry. As we stated in the beginning of this chapter, if you want to know the temperature of an organization, stick the thermometer in the leader's mouth. Did you know this is true of the various aspects of the organization as well? For instance:

- If you want to know the evangelistic temperature of a Sunday School class, stick the evangelistic thermometer in the teacher's mouth.
- If you want to know the ministry temperature of a Sunday School class, stick the ministry thermometer in the teacher's mouth.

- If you want to know the discipleship temperature of a Sunday School class, stick the discipleship thermometer in the teacher's mouth.
- If you want to know the friendly temperature of a Sunday School class, stick the friendly thermometer in the teacher's mouth.

The leader sets the bar for "organizational atmosphere." The Sunday School organization will be as warm, friendly, inviting, and accepting as the Sunday School leader. Organizations take on the personality of their leader. When I teach our Potential Teacher Class, I instruct our prospective teachers that their class will only be as friendly as they are. It may take a little time, but eventually a class will take on the personality of the teacher. If I attend a class and the members are not friendly, then I know the teacher is not friendly. Many of our classes would grow if people would simply befriend those who attend.

The leader sets the bar for "organizational atmosphere."

Some of my staff and I did a weekend conference for a church in another state. As we were driving back home, they were commenting how the people at the church were unfriendly. This was a good church, but I had to agree with them. After listening for a while, I commented, "Do you know why they are unfriendly?'

"No," they said, "do you have a thought?"

"Yes," I replied, "their pastor was unfriendly."

They quickly shot back, "How do you know? He wasn't even there."

"O yes, he was there," I said. "Did he speak to any of you?"

"No," they replied. "He never spoke to me either," I said.

This was not a bad church. They were preaching the gospel and teaching the Bible, but they were not friendly. Many Sunday School classes are like this. They have great Bible study and wonderful koinonia with existing members, but newcomers are not made to feel welcome.

Three words ought to be in the minds of every leader and teacher when they are at church. These three important words are *speak*, *smile*, and *touch*. What do they have in common? They reveal the consideration given others. When you speak, smile, and touch, you express interest in the other person.

We must use discretion when it comes to touching, but an appropriate touch can mean so much. One Sunday morning I spoke to a lady in our church who is a widow. As I did, I gave her a hug. She thanked me with tears in her eyes for the hug and shared, "As a widow, I go all week without a physical touch of affection." Often Jesus would heal people by touching them. Have you ever wondered why He would touch them when He could just speak the word and immediately healing would take place? In His wisdom He chose to touch people. I am of the opinion that He wanted people to be made whole, but He also wanted them to feel the touch of His love.

Some leaders may say that they are introverted and are not comfortable speaking, smiling, and touching. My advice is to get over it! Leaders do not do things for their comfort or benefit; they do them for the benefit of others! Come on leader, recognize your role! I try to speak, smile, and touch everyone that makes eye contact with me. I do this even if I do not know the person because everyone ought to be encouraged by receiving a little attention. It only takes two seconds to do it. The interest you express to others brings warmth to their soul. This is one of the things that so impresses me with Jesus. He was always picking up those who were down. He was always adding value to people. Jesus was in the people business, and a Sunday School leader in HD will do the same.

Every Sunday School needs standards, direction, and atmosphere. Atmosphere is the heart of the organization; direction is the soul of the organization; and standards are the mind of the organization. A Sunday School in HD will have heart, soul, and mind!

Leadership Is Stewardship

The Bible instructs us to be good stewards.

> Let a man so consider us, as servants of Christ and stewards of the mysteries of God. Moreover it is required in stewards that one be found faithful. (1 Cor. 4:1–2)

> As each one has received a gift, minister it to one another, as good stewards of the manifold grace of God. (1 Pet. 4:10)

Being a good steward is necessary for all Christians, but especially Christian leaders, because Christian leaders influence others. There are people whose spiritual well-being lies within the realm of our influence. We cannot and we must not take this lightly.

One morning during my quiet time I was having a new thought. I was meditating on stewardship in a way that really intrigued me. When we think of stewardship, usually the first thing that pops into our mind is money, so we give consideration to how we can better manage our finances. As we think further about stewardship, the second thought that comes to mind is time, so we give careful attention to how we can better direct our time. On this morning my new thought moved me to deliberate on the stewardship of my influence. I had never contemplated that thought in my life. As I reflected on that, I came to realize that the stewardship of influence is a greater responsibility than the stewardship of my money and time. I reasoned that the stewardship of my money and time mostly affected me, but the stewardship of my influence

> **The stewardship of influence is a greater responsibility than the stewardship of my money and time.**

affected others. That morning I wrote down several conclusions that I came to believe and now keep in the front of my Bible.

Influence is a good thing to have.

Now, it can be exerted in a bad way. Adolph Hitler had influence, but he used it wrongly. Nevertheless, influence is still a good thing and should be used rightly.

Influence is a good gift to have, and good gifts are given by God.

> Every good gift and every perfect gift is from above, and comes down from the Father of lights, with whom there is no variation or shadow of turning." (James 1:17)

Since God has given me influence, then I should not be afraid to exercise it.

If God gave it to me then, He expects me to use it and will hold me accountable for it. If God gifts us with a great singing voice, He expects us to use it for His glory. If God gives me money, then He expects me to use it for His kingdom. The same is true if He bestows influence upon us.

Influence should be exercised within the confines of the fruit of the Spirit.

> But the fruit of the Spirit is love, joy, peace, longsuffering, kindness, goodness, faithfulness, gentleness, self-control. Against such there is no law. (Gal. 5:22–23)

The fruit of the Spirit operates as guardrails in our lives to keep us on the right road and out of the ditch. We do not have the right to exercise our influence over others in a selfish or arrogant way. Every gift should be exercised within the context of the fruit of the Spirit. The fruit of the Spirit in your life is more important than the gifts of the Spirit in your life. A leader devoid of the fruit of the Spirit will negate the gifts of the Spirit. Paul made this abundantly clear to the church at Corinth.

> Though I speak with the tongues of men and of angels, but *have not love*, I have become sounding brass or a clanging cymbal. And though I have the gift of prophecy, and understand all mysteries and all knowledge, and though I have all faith, so that I could remove mountains, but *have not love*, I am nothing. And though I bestow all my goods to feed the poor, and though I give my body to be burned, but *have not love*, it profits me nothing. (1 Cor. 13:1–3, *emphasis mine*)

Leaders are influencers and must be good stewards of that influence. Sunday School leadership is paramount in a high-definition Sunday School. Lead her well!

CHAPTER 10

G-R-E-A-T Leaders

Leadership is so vital in producing Sunday Schools that are vibrant and growing. Great leaders are highly defined leaders that produce highly defined organizations. Every Sunday School leader should strive to be a great leader. Some may argue that this exposes pride. I would ask, "What's the alternative?" If you do not want to be a great leader, then do you aspire to be a sorry leader? Of course you do not. God wants you to be the very best you can be. There are five basic attributes of G–R–E–A–T leaders.

- **G**odly
- **R**elational
- **E**xpert
- **A**ction-oriented
- **T**hinker

Godly (Key Word: Character)

Sunday School leaders are to be godly first and foremost. Being a Sunday School leader is not about popularity or power in the church. It is not a position to exalt; it is a service to render. It is not a position to take so people can think highly of you; it is a position to take so you can think highly of others as you serve them. Some people take places of leadership because it provides a platform for their self-serving agenda.

> **Sunday School leaders are to be godly first and foremost.**

This was the case of the Pharisees. They were egotistical and loved the place of power, prestige, and prominence. They would not relinquish their exalted position because it served their own pride. We see this played out immediately after Jesus had raised Lazarus from the dead.

> Then many of the Jews who had come to Mary, and had seen the things Jesus did, believed in Him. But some of them went away to the Pharisees and told them the things Jesus did. Then the chief priests and the Pharisees gathered a council and said, "What shall we do? For this Man works many signs. If we let Him alone like this, everyone will believe in Him, and the Romans will come and *take away both our place and nation*." (John 11:45–48, *emphasis mine*)

These religious leaders were envious of Jesus. People actually wanted to follow Him instead of them. They were losing their influence and could not handle it. The Gospel of Mark records the real motive behind them taking Jesus to Pilate.

> But Pilate answered them, saying, "Do you want me to release to you the King of the Jews?" *For he knew that the chief priests had handed Him over because of envy.* But the chief priests stirred up the crowd, so that he should rather release Barabbas to them." (Mark 15:9–11, *emphasis mine*)

The Pharisees were leaders with impure motives. Their intentions were self-serving. Leaders beware. We should serve with wholesome motives. Leaders are to serve the position and the people; the position is not to serve them. Leaders are to serve the church not vice versa.

A godly Sunday School leader should be *holy.* One cannot be godly without being holy. The more holy we are the more like God we become. If I could only use one word to describe God, I would choose *holy.* He is holy, and He wants us to be like Him.

> But as He who called you is holy, you also be holy in all your conduct; because it is written, "Be holy, for I am holy." (1 Pet. 1:15–16)

A godly Sunday School leader should be *humble.* I believe humility produces holiness because God cannot make you holy until you first humble yourself. The old cliché is true; the way up is down.

> Likewise you younger people, submit yourselves to your elders. Yes, all of you be submissive to one another, and be clothed with humility, for "God resists the proud, but gives grace to the humble." Therefore humble yourselves under the mighty hand of God, that He may exalt you in due time. (1 Pet. 5:5–6)

I want to be able to live and minister without resistance, but if resistance must come, I certainly do not want it coming from God! And pride will cause God to resist me.

If I could only use one word to describe Satan, I would choose *pride.* What is pride? It is being full of yourself, and that describes Satan. Right in the middle of pride is a big *I*—p-r-**I**-d-e. And right in the middle of sin is a big *I*—s-**I**-n.

> "How are you fallen from heaven, O Lucifer, son of the morning! How you are cut down to the ground, You who weakened the nations! For you have said in your heart: '*I will* ascend into heaven, *I will* exalt

> my throne about the stars of God; *I will* also sit on the mount of the congregation on the farthest sides of the north; *I will* ascend about the heights of the clouds, *I will* be like the Most High.' Yet you shall be brought down to Sheol, to the lowest depths of the Pit." (Isa. 14:12–15, *emphasis mine*)

Five times Satan says, "I will." Each "I will" exposes his pride as he seeks a position that does not belong to him but belongs to God and God alone! His pride crescendos until his last "I will" proclaims, "I will be like the Most High!" What pride Satan has, what ego, what arrogance, what conceit, and what sin!

This is completely opposite of Jesus. He did not say, "I will," but rather, "Your will."

> He went a little farther and fell on His face, and prayed, saying, "O My Father, if it is possible, let this cup pass from Me; nevertheless, not as I will, but as You will. " (Matt. 26:39)

A humble Sunday School leader will be like Jesus, doing the Father's will, not his own will. I cannot find anywhere in Scripture where Jesus announced His character traits. He does not say that He is a man of great character, integrity, wisdom, love, etc. The one character trait He does publicize is His meekness and lowliness.

> "Take My yoke upon you and learn from Me, for I am gentle and lowly in heart, and you will find rest for your souls." (Matt. 11:29)

God hates pride more than any other sin. It was the sin that caused Lucifer to fall from heaven. It was the sin with which Satan tempted Eve. Satan wanted to be God then deceived Eve by telling her that she would be "like God."

> Now the serpent was more cunning than any beast of the field which the LORD God had made. And he

> said to the woman, "Has God indeed said, 'You shall not eat of every tree of the garden'?" And the woman said to the serpent, "We may eat the fruit of the trees of the garden; but of the fruit of the tree which is in the midst of the garden, God has said, 'You shall not eat it, nor shall you touch it, lest you die.'" Then the serpent said to the woman, "You will not surely die. For God knows that in the day you eat of it your eyes will be opened, and you will be like God, knowing good and evil." (Gen. 3:1–5, *emphasis mine*)

In Proverbs 6 the Bible says that seven things are an abomination to God, and the first thing mentioned is "a proud look." The Bible has much to say about pride and a haughty spirit and none of it is good.

A godly Sunday School leader should be *hungry.*

> "Blessed are those who hunger and thirst for righteousness." (Matt. 5:6)

A church leader should be hungry for righteousness, and Sunday School leaders are church leaders. Nobody gets a thirty-minute platform with the people each week except the pastor and the Sunday School teachers. If we are really hungry for righteousness, then we will want to be in church and hear Bible sermons and lessons; we will want to have a personal, daily quiet time to get alone to pray and read God's Word; we will want to flee those things that are unrighteous.

Relational (Key Word: Caring)

Sunday School leaders should want to have relationships with those they serve, and they should want to lead from those relationships. People will follow those that genuinely care for them. As shepherds, leaders should know their sheep and desire the best for them. Some have said that church leaders should be like a CEO, implying that the biblical illustration of a shepherd is no longer relevant. May

I say, "it isn't so." If that were true, then the Bible has portions that are no longer pertinent. Leaders are shepherds who spend time with their sheep and know their sheep.

> Be diligent to know the state of your flocks, and attend to your herds." (Prov. 27:23)

The Bible gives us some wonderful examples of those who led from their relationship. I want to share three illustrations of godly leaders exercising leadership with great care for the sheep they were leading.

> So they brought the ark of the Lord, and set it in its place in the midst of the tabernacle that David had erected for it. Then David offered burnt offerings and peace offerings before the Lord. And when David had finished offering burnt offerings and peace offerings, he blessed the people in the name of the Lord of hosts. Then he distributed among all the people, among the whole multitude of Israel, both the women and the men, to everyone a loaf of bread, a piece of meat, and a cake of raisins. So all the people departed, everyone to his house. Then David returned to bless his household. And Michal the daughter of Saul came out to meet David, and said, "How glorious was the king of Israel today, uncovering himself today in the eyes of the maids of his servants, as one of the base fellows shamelessly uncovers himself!" So David said to Michal, "It was before the Lord, who chose me instead of your father and all his house, to appoint me ruler over the people of the Lord, over Israel. Therefore, I will play music before the Lord. And I will be even more undignified than this, and will be humble in my own sight. But as for the maidservants of whom you have spoken, by them I will be held in honor."

> Therefore Michal the daughter of Saul had no children to the day of her death. (2 Sam. 6:17–23)

David did two things as a shepherd of the people. First, he fed them. Shepherds feed sheep. Scripture indicates there was a great crowd of people. It must have been expensive for David to underwrite this meal. Next, he worshipped and danced with the people before the Lord. He was not too good to be with them and associate with them. He actually believed it would bring him honor to do so!

We see a second example of relational leadership in Paul. A slave named Onesimus had apparently run away from his master, Philemon. Paul got acquainted with him and led him to faith in Christ. He then writes Philemon asking him to receive Onesimus back in kindness. Notice how he beseeches Philemon with much gentleness and love.

> Therefore, though I might be very bold in Christ to command you what is fitting, yet for love's sake I rather appeal to you—being such a one as Paul, the aged, and now also a prisoner of Jesus Christ—I appeal to you for my son Onesimus, whom I have begotten while in my chains. . . . whom I wished to keep with me, that on your behalf he might minister to me in my chains for the gospel. But without your consent I wanted to do nothing, that your good deed might not be by compulsion, as it were, but voluntary. . . . If then you count me as a partner, receive him as you would me. . . . Yes, brother, let me have joy from you in the Lord; refresh my heart in the Lord. Having confidence in your obedience, I write to you, knowing that you will do even more than I say. (Philem. 8–10, 13–14, 17, 20–21)

It would be easy to say that since Paul was one of the apostles and the church was built on the foundation of the apostles, he should have put his foot down and told Philemon what to do. He should have exerted his apostolic leadership and demanded that Philemon fall in line with it. Yet he entreated Philemon as a dearly beloved brother. Why? He had a relationship with him.

The last example comes as Peter, another apostle, teaches church leaders how to exercise their authority.

> The elders who are among you I exhort, I who am a fellow elder and a witness of the sufferings of Christ, and also a partaker of the glory that will be revealed: Shepherd the flock of God which is among you, serving as overseers, not by compulsion but willingly, not for dishonest gain but eagerly; nor as being lords over those entrusted to you, but being examples to the flock. (1 Pet. 5:1–3)

Peter was one of only three men who had seen the glory of the Lord as He was transfigured on the high mountain. Not only was he one of three men to see the Christ transfigured; he saw Moses and Elijah too. How would you like to have that on your resume? Yet Peter did not strut his stuff. He said they were not to lord it over the sheep but rather to be examples for them to follow.

I am impressed with these three biblical and spiritual giants. They were great leaders partly because they knew how to handle people.

Expert (Key Word: Competent)

I believe every person who takes a position of leadership should be an expert in that position or soon become one. I have never seen the position of "good ole boy" in the church, yet we often think that is all it takes to fill the position. There is nothing wrong with being a good ole boy, but that in and of itself is insufficient to get the ministry accomplished. It takes more than drinking coffee and slapping someone on the back to move Sunday School forward.

If we are doing something for the Lord, should we not strive to be as skillful as we can? Are we not supposed to give our best to God? My favorite leadership verse in the Bible is Psalm 78:72.

> "So he (David) shepherded them according to the integrity of his heart, and guided them by the skillfulness of his hands."

This speaks of David's godliness and character. It also speaks of his skill and competency. This is a powerful combination for any leader. If you do not possess godliness, the people will not let you lead them. If you do not possess competency, you cannot lead them. It takes both qualities. Most recognize the need to be godly; fewer recognize the need to be skillful. This is why churches are full of leaders (both staff leaders and lay leaders) who have godliness but possess little skill. The difference is that churches will not tolerate ungodliness, but they will stomach incompetency. The truth is that a void of either keeps one from leading.

The church has tolerated mediocrity too long. When I hire staff members, I tell them that they are to be experts in the area of ministry to which they are employed. If they are not experts, then we have the wrong person. Our staff reads a book a month to sharpen our skill level continually. Likewise, a Sunday School teacher or leader should take advantage of all the books, conferences, and training that he can. If a Sunday School teacher or leader is unwilling to continue the process of ministry growth, then he should step down. God's people deserve the best we can give them, and God deserves the best we can give Him.

God's people deserve the best we can give them, and God deserves the best we can give Him.

As a young man in ministry, Timothy received this kind of mentoring from Paul. Paul wanted Timothy to continue to grow, develop his gifts, and be a better leader.

> Till I come, give attention to reading, to exhortation, to doctrine. Do not neglect the gift that is in you, which was given to you by prophecy with the laying on of the hands of the eldership. Meditate on these things; give yourself entirely to them, that your progress may be evident to all. Take heed to yourself and to the doctrine. Continue in them, for in doing this you will save both yourself and those who hear you." (1 Tim. 4:13–16)

I want us to see several things that Paul instructed Timothy.

- "Give attention to"—Pay attention and put focus on reading the Bible and learning doctrine.
- "Meditate on these things"—Think about these things and reflect on them constantly.
- "Give yourself entirely to them"—Be dedicated to your ministry and the things of it.
- "That your progress may be evident to all"—People ought to see your growth and improvement.
- "Take heed to yourself"—Watch after yourself and be concerned with who you are and what you are becoming.
- "Continue in them"—Continue to grow in your knowledge of the teachings of Scripture.
- "For in doing this you will save both yourself and those who hear you"—Not only are you dependent upon your growth, but so are those you lead.

Action-oriented (Key Word: Commitment)

The Sunday School leader must be a person of action. The purpose of leadership is to get something done, and this requires action. A person of action will be known as an initiator. He does not stand around with his hands in his pocket hoping for something to take place. He takes it upon himself to make something happen. The leader is the rock that hits the pond and creates the first ripple. The first ripple then spreads and creates the second ripple, which creates the third ripple, etc. If there is no rock there will be no ripples. Too many Sunday Schools are like a smooth, glassy pond. There has not been a ripple there in years. We just sit idly by not realizing we are the rock. Even the four lepers in 2 Kings 7:3–4 knew better than this.

The purpose of leadership is to get something done, and this requires action.

> Four men with skin diseases were at the entrance to the gate. They said to each other, "Why just sit here until we die? If we say, 'Let's go into the city,' we will die there because the famine is in the city, but if we sit here, we will also die. So now, come on. Let's go to the Arameans' camp. If they let us live, we will live; if they kill us, we will die." (HCSB)

Sunday Schools are sitting around, dying of leprosy, and doing nothing about it. You have to do something. The lepers knew they were at the point that they had to try something. The good news was that it did not even matter if their idea failed because they were doomed anyway if they did nothing. Leaders, take counsel. Has your Sunday School been in decline or plateaued for some time? Then what are you going to do about it? Do not just sit there, you have got to do something! As the initiator, the rock, go create some ripples. I have found that it is better for the leader to be a little too aggressive than to be a little too passive.

A leader of action is also decisive. Leaders have to make decisions. Obviously you will want to gather important facts and look for the right timing, but eventually you have to make a call. Joshua was this kind of leader, and he longed to surround himself with others that were decisive.

> "And if it seems evil to you to serve the Lord, choose for yourselves this day whom you will serve, whether the gods which your fathers served that were on the other side of the River, or the gods of the Amorites, in whose land you dwell. But as for me and my house, we will serve the Lord." (Josh. 24:15)

Joshua challenged the people to pick a god to serve even if it was not Jehovah God. As a leader he was decisive, and he prompted the people to be decisive as well. It has been said that the best thing you can do is to make the right decision. The second best thing you can do is to make the wrong decision. The worst thing you can do is to make no decision.

Thinker (Key Word: Considerate)

I am greatly concerned for America because we are a people who have quit thinking. We are so entertainment driven that we allow the television to do all our thinking for us. This has greatly affected our society and, consequently, the church as well. I am amazed at what we buy into without really thinking it through. King David was a thinker. As he sat in the fields watching sheep, he must have done a lot of thinking and developed this discipline in his life.

> I remember the days of old; I meditate on all Your works; I muse on the work of Your hands." (Ps. 143:5)

David used the word *muse* which *Strong's Exhaustive Concordance* defines "to ponder, to converse with oneself, to meditate." This is the only place the word is used in the Bible. Placing the letter "a" before a word negates the word. Thus, muse would become *amuse*, meaning to not ponder or meditate. Today we have our *amusement* parks. This is not a place where great thinking takes place. You just show up and have fun because everything is already thought through for you. It seems that believers have been influenced by our culture. We show up at church desiring *amusement* instead of *musement.*

David was a thinker and spent time doing just that.

> Now it came to pass when the king was *dwelling in his house*, and the LORD had given him rest from all his enemies all around, that the king said to Nathan the prophet, "See now, I dwell in a house of cedar, but the ark of God dwells inside tent curtains." (2 Sam. 7:1–2, *emphasis mine*)

David was in his house and was obviously thinking. He thought it was not right that he should live in a nice house while the ark of covenant was housed in a tent. He wanted to build a temple for the ark of God. God reserved that for David's son, Solomon, but the idea of a temple was born in the heart of David as he *mused*. Then God, through the prophet Nathan, gave him what we know as the Davidic Covenant. This again caused David to ponder and meditate as he "sat before the Lord."

> Then King David went in and *sat before the LORD*; and he said, "Who am I, O Lord GOD? And what is my house, that You have brought me this far?" (2 Sam. 7:18, *emphasis mine*)

Too many leaders spend too little time thinking through issues. As a result, we are left to do nothing but chase every trend and every fad that comes down the pike. Many of these are good and will be helpful. However, some may not be a good fit for your church setting. In the Great Commandment Jesus encouraged us to be *musers*.

> Jesus said to him, "You shall love the LORD your God with all your heart, with all your soul, and with all your *mind*. This is the first and great commandment." (Matt. 22:37–38, *emphasis mine*)

We are to love God *devotionally*—"with all your heart." We are to love God *volitionally*—"with all your soul." We are also to love God *intellectually*—"with all your mind." Dear friend, it is a sin not to love God with your mind. Remember, in this passage Jesus gave us the Great Commandment, not a thought-provoking suggestion. A nonthinking Sunday School leader may ignite the dynamite under his own organization.

It is a sin not to love God with your mind.

Sunday School leaders must think about many issues. What are you trying to accomplish through your Sunday School ministry? How does your class time support the mission of your Sunday School? What is your process of enlisting and equipping leaders? What do you expect from your leaders? Why do you use the curriculum you do? A *musing* Sunday School leader thinks over these issues and leads with character and competency. An *amusing* leader neglects his thinking duty and ultimately watches as the Sunday School ministry fizzles out all the while wondering how it happened.

I want to provide one practical exercise for thinking Sunday School leaders. I have a great uneasiness that we are not as concerned for children as we should be. We may differ on our views, but we must think through three key issues regarding our precious children. The first concern is that some churches do not provide a small group Bible study experience for children. Many of these churches use the method of home cell groups instead of a traditional Sunday School. Oftentimes, home groups must provide babysitters to care for their children while they are meeting. When they attend church on Sundays, some have children's church while the adults attend their worship service. In this scenario their children are never in a small group Bible study where an adult pours biblical truth into these moldable little minds. I must be honest in saying that one word describes my feeling on this—tragic! As a Christian educator I am more committed to children receiving a small group experience than even the adults. It seems that the focus today is on adults and not children, yet the majority of believers come to Christ as children. If small groups are important, then should they not be important for children?

> **If small groups are important, then should they not be important for children?**

Second, I am concerned that some churches do not provide a forum for children to hear their pastor. Some churches have programmed children away from their pastor. Many deem the worship service to be at a level that is out of range for a child. This is true to some degree, but if this same rationale were applied to secular education, no one would ever attend chemistry and calculus classes. Everyone needs to be in an environment that stretches us and teaches us things we did not know. Furthermore, children miss the teachings that come from symbolism such as the Lord's Supper and baptism. I think it is important for children to hear their pastor, know him, and grow to respect the man of God. How can a child call a man their pastor when they never see him or know who he is?

Third, I am concerned that some churches do not provide opportunities for families to worship together. The number one spiritual influence in a child's life is his parents. Yet the church has established programs so that a child and his parents are never together at church. Let me state the obvious: God gave children to parents! God did not give children to churches or Christian schools. The church experience is probably the apex of a family's weekly spiritual practice, yet individual family members are separated from one another the entire time they attend church. I certainly understand the need for churches to offer age-appropriate programs and events, but do we offer so many that children are always detached from their parents? It is important for children to see their parents worshipping God, singing praises to God, dropping their offering in the offering plate, praying, following the pastor with an open Bible, etc. Learning is both educational and experiential. When children attend an age-appropriate small group Bible study, they receive educational learning; when they attend worship with their parents, they receive experiential learning. Many contend that it is unsuitable for a child to attend "big church," and the church is in error to expect otherwise. If that is the case, then the people of God did it wrong from the time corporate worship started until the 1960s. Are we to assume that for about six thousand years the people of God were mistaken on this? In the Bible we see families worshipping together. If this was inappropriate, surely some godly leader would have spoken against it, and yet we have no record that one did.

> **God gave children to parents! God did not give children to churches or Christian schools.**

The three issues mentioned must be thought through by church leaders. They are important issues. These issues are a challenge for any church but especially for churches that use small groups in homes rather than Sunday School. I do not say this in opposition to cell churches. It is never wrong for a small group to gather for Bible study, prayer, fellowship, etc. Furthermore, many churches, especially new church plants, have little choice because of facilities. Every decision has some trade-offs, and we need to understand what they are and make decisions accordingly.

Great Sunday Schools have G–R–E–A–T leaders. If we are to define Sunday School with the clarity she needs, then it will take G–R–E–A–T leaders paving the way.

CHAPTER 11

Keeping Our Sacred Trust

When a person accepts a position of church leadership, they assume a sacred trust with God and with those they are to lead. Every follower wants to be assured that his leader is keeping his sacred trust. Spiritual leadership is not to be entered into lightly. There is a cost to count, and there is a responsibility to bear. Writing to his young mentee, Paul makes a profound statement about his ministry and his responsibility with it.

> According to the glorious gospel of the blessed God which was *committed to my trust.* (1 Tim. 1:11, *emphasis mine*)

Paul concludes his first pastoral epistle to his protégé with a statement about Timothy's ministry and his responsibility to it.

> O Timothy! Guard what was *committed to your trust.* (1 Tim. 6:20, *emphasis mine*)

I remember when my first child, Kelly, was born. I was so proud to show her to family and friends who dropped by the hospital and to pass out bubble gum cigars. This went on for three days, and then the hospital personnel said it was time to take her home. Take her home! What was I going to do with her? Linda and I had never had a baby before, and the thoughts of taking her home were very frightening. As I loaded the car, I remember thinking, *What in the world am I going to do? This isn't a piece of furniture that could be replaced if it broke. This is a real, live human being, and I am responsible for her!* God had blessed me with her and placed her in my hand. He had committed her to my sacred trust!

Sunday School leaders have been committed to a sacred trust. Each week Sunday School teachers handle the two most precious things to God: His Word and His people! I do not know of anything that God loves more than His Word and His people, and He has entrusted them to our sacred trust. This ought to create much soberness about us—much seriousness about us, and much single-mindedness about us.

Spiritually speaking, the world has gone to sleep. The devil has even lured the church into slumber with his deceptive lullabies. He has gotten the church yawning! The church has so mingled with the world that we can hardly tell the difference between the two! Is it fair to say that the majority of churches are struggling? Plateaued? Declining? Is it valid to say that the majority of believers live mediocre Christian lives? Is it true that we have more lukewarm Christianity today than ever before? Is it fair to say that the church of Jesus Christ is not as vibrant as we should be? Could it be that Sunday School leaders are sleeping on the job?

> **Sunday School leaders have been committed to a sacred trust.**

Instructions to watch, be spiritually alert, and be sober-minded are given throughout the Bible.

> Therefore gird up the loins of your mind, *be sober.* (1 Pet. 1:13, *emphasis mine*)

> But the end of all things is at hand; therefore be *serious* and *watchful* in your prayers. (1 Pet. 4:7, *emphasis mine*)

> Be *sober*, be vigilant; because your adversary the devil walks about like a roaring lion, seeking whom he may devour. (1 Pet. 5:8, *emphasis mine*)

The Bible is full of Scriptural references about being spiritually alert and sober. God wants to get our attention and put us on guard spiritually. He wants us to be committed to our sacred trust. He wants us to be spiritually alert in handling those sacred responsibilities endowed by Him.

Four Aspects of "Keeping Our Sacred Trust"

I want to pose four questions to help us consider the keeping of our sacred trust.

1. Are we asleep to our commission?

The number one reason Jesus came to earth was for the salvation of souls. He did many great things while He was here like teaching God's truth, healing sick people, and even raising people from the dead. However, it is evident from His own words that nothing could unseat His priority of seeing people converted.

> Jesus told them, "For the Son of Man has come to seek and to save the lost." (Luke 19:10 HCSB)

> "I have come that they may have life and have it in abundance." (John 10:10 HCSB)

Paul and Peter both would later weigh in on Christ's priority.

> "This is good, and it pleases God our Savior, who wants everyone saved and to come to the knowledge of the truth." (1 Tim. 2:3–4 HCSB)

> The Lord does not delay His promise, as some understand delay, but is patient with you, not wanting any to perish, but all to come to repentance. (2 Pet. 3:9 HCSB)

The church should align her priority with that of Jesus. The question that must be asked is, "Does the modern-day church have the same priority as Jesus?" If we do not, then we have fallen asleep to our commission. I recently attended a small group conference where attendees were asked to vote on what was the number one priority of small groups. Each of the twelve hundred or so attendees selected from the list that was made up of worship, evangelism, discipleship, ministry, and fellowship. When the vote was taken, only one person selected evangelism as the number one priority of small groups. This greatly troubled me because it exposed that we are not asleep to our commission; we are in a coma!

The church should align her priority with that of Jesus.

I recently conducted a survey of 1,517 Sunday School leaders. These people were not just regular Sunday School members; they were teachers and leaders in the Sunday School ministry of their local church. I asked them to list the first, second, and third priorities of Sunday School from a list that included Bible study, fellowship, prayer, worship, meeting needs, outreach, and assimilation. Here are the results of the first-place votes.

Category	Total Votes	Percentage
Bible Study	1,082	71%
Outreach	208	14%
Meeting Needs	109	7%
Fellowship	61	4%
Worship	30	2%
Assimilation	17	1%
Prayer	10	1%

Again, this was bothersome to think that only 14 percent of Sunday School leaders would list evangelism (outreach) as the number one priority of Sunday School. In both of these experiences, I felt that Bible study or discipleship would get the majority of votes, but I did not believe the gap would be so great between it and evangelism. Let me offer some statistical evidence from the Annual Church Profiles of my own Southern Baptist Convention that demonstrates we have fallen asleep to our commission.

- From 2004 to 2007 Sunday School enrollment decreased 329,829.
- From 2004 to 2007 baptisms declined 42,006.
- From 2004 to 2007 youth baptisms dropped 8,051.
- In 2007 only 102 churches out of over 45,000 baptized as many as thirty-three teenagers.

Parable of the Fishermen (From *Church Growth: American Magazine*, September/October 1978)

Now it came to pass that a group existed who called themselves fishermen. And lo, there were many fish in the waters all around. In fact, the whole area was surrounded by streams and lakes filled with fish. And the fish were hungry.

Week after week, month after month, and year after year, these who called themselves fishermen met in meetings and talked about their call to go about fishing.

Continually they searched for new and better methods of fishing and for new and better definitions of fishing. They sponsored costly nationwide and worldwide congresses to discuss fishing, to promote fishing, and to hear about all the ways of fishing, such as the new fishing equipment, fish calls, and the discovery of any new bait.

These fishermen built large, beautiful buildings called "Fishing Headquarters." The plea was that everyone should be a fishermen and every fishermen should fish. There was one thing they didn't do, however; they didn't fish.

All the fishermen seemed to agree that what was needed was a board which could challenge fishermen to be faithful in fishing. The board was formed by those who had the great vision and courage to speak about fishing, to define fishing, and to promote the idea of fishing in far-away streams and lakes where many other fish of different colors lived.

Large elaborate and expensive training centers were built with the purpose of teaching fishermen how to fish. Those who taught had doctorates in fishology. But the teachers did not fish. They only taught fishing.

Some spent much study and travel to learn the history of fishing and to see far-away places where the founding fathers did great fishing in the centuries past. They lauded the faithful fishermen of years before who handed down the idea of fishing.

Many who felt the call to be fishermen responded. They were commissioned and sent to fish. And they went off to foreign lands . . . to teach fishing.

Now it's true that many of the fishermen sacrificed and put up with all kinds of difficulties. Some lived near the water and bore the smell of dead fish every day. They received the ridicule of some who made fun of their fishermen's clubs. They anguished over those who were not committed enough to attend

> the weekly meetings to talk about fishing. After all, were they not following the Master who said, "Follow me and I will make you fishers of men"?
>
> Imagine how hurt some were when one day a person suggested that those who don't catch fish were really not fishermen, no matter how much they claimed to be. Yet it did sound correct. Is a person a fisherman if year after year he/she never catches a fish? Is one following if he isn't fishing? (Copyright 2000 by Chick Publications–Battle Cry Newsletter. Web site: www.chick.com. Used by permission.)

This parable looks a lot like our Sunday Schools. We teach fishing, but we never go fishing. We study much on the topic of fishing, but we never go to the riverbank and cast our bait. Our command is to "go," and the Sunday School leader must keep his sacred trust to lead a going Sunday School because reaching people is not a question of convenience but of divine compulsion!

We teach fishing, but we never go fishing.

> Then the master said to the servant, "Go out into the highways and hedges, and compel them to come in, that my house may be filled." (Luke 14:23)

Forty-two times in the Gospel of John alone Jesus referred to the fact that He was "sent" from the Father. After His resurrection He closes out the Gospel by commissioning us as His sent ones.

> So Jesus said to them again, "Peace to you! As the Father has sent Me, I also send you." And when He had said this, He breathed on them, and said to them, "Receive the Holy Spirit. If you forgive the sins of any, they are forgiven them; if you retain the sins of any, they are retained." (John 20:21–23)

2. Are we adrift to our convictions?

Political correctness has flowed like a stream into the pond of religion. Religious waters have been so tainted by political correctness that it has produced religious correctness. Many pastors are afraid to proclaim the exclusivity of Jesus as the only way to heaven. Some of them have even become television celebrities and best-selling authors. The tragedy in America, however, is not our political correctness; it is our religious correctness. We have replaced what God says with what man thinks. In the beginning God created us in His image; ever since, we have been trying to create Him in our image! There is a huge difference between the *God we want* versus the *God who is*! Understand that there is no need for the good news if there were not first "bad news."

The polluted waters of political and religious correctness have now flowed into the pond of leadership and have fashioned "leadership correctness." Truth has never been more compromised than today. We have sacrificed truth on the altar of compatibility. In our effort to make everyone feel good, we have often rendered our leadership ineffective by seeking middle ground over the high ground. Leadership correctness seeks popularity with people and has replaced power with God. A Spirit-led, Spirit-illuminated Sunday School leader will not treasure good feelings over good theology. I am not suggesting looking for a fight every week in Sunday School, nor am I suggesting insensitivity to people. What I am suggesting is the instruction of Paul when he told the church at Ephesus to speak "the truth in love," (Eph. 4:15). The leader must cling to conviction when no one else does if he is to keep his ministry healthy. To lose your convictions is to lose your right to lead. A leader must value his values. If he does not value his values, then he is no longer valuable. Furthermore, if he does not value his values, then he does not even value himself.

To lose your convictions is to lose your right to lead.

Conviction is found in the Word of God. A spiritual leader must spend daily time in the Bible. The Bible is replete with illustrations showing that spiritual leaders were men of the Word. They were biblical students that read, studied, and meditated on Scripture. They were not biblical sluggards as we see in "The 23rd Channel."

The 23rd Channel
(Author Unknown)

The TV is my shepherd, I shall not want.
It makes me lie down on the sofa.
It leads me away from the scriptures.
It destroys my soul.
It leads me in the path of sex and violence for the sponsor's sake.
Yea, though I walk in the shadow of my Christian responsibilities,
There will be no interruption
For the TV is with me.
Its cable and remote control, they comfort me.
It prepares a commercial before me in the presence of my worldliness.
It anoints my head with humanism.
My coveting runneth over.
Surely laziness and ignorance shall follow me all the days of my life;
And I shall dwell in the house watching TV forever.
(www.bibleplace.com/p23pslm.htm)

A Sunday School ministry cannot impact this dark, evil world if her members are not biblically prepared. Yet, when members of cults knock on our doors, evangelical church members run and hide under the bed until they leave because we have not biblically prepared ourselves. We have not heeded the admonition of Peter.

> But sanctify the Lord God in your hearts, and always be ready to give a defense to everyone who asks you a reason for the hope that is in you, with meekness and fear." (1 Pet. 3:15)

There is no way we can have a Sunday School in HD if we do not have definition on the most critical issue—the truth! Sunday School leaders must keep their sacred trust by upholding biblical convictions.

3. Are we apathetic to our calling?

Spiritual leaders cannot, they must not, grow cold and apathetic to their spiritual duty. They should be hot hearted and enthusiastic about God's calling on their lives. I get weary with spiritual leaders who mope around sulking over their responsibilities. Everyone carries a heavy weight from time to time, but I find great difficulty accepting leaders who are infected with the martyr syndrome. "Woe is me" is their constant motto. If it is true that God is always with us and that He called us into this service, then straighten up those slumping shoulders, put resolve in your heart, and serve God with joy.

Over these years of ministry at First Baptist Woodstock, I have grown to love my pastor deeply. I will do whatever he asks of me because I love him and believe in him. Not only will I serve him, but my love for him will also cause me to serve him with enthusiasm and passion. I do not dread his asking something of me; rather, I am pleased when he does. A leader should have this attitude and even better as he serves God. God loves us and has called us into His service. We should serve Him with joy and enthusiasm, not as some sacrificial victim. In fact, nothing should put passion into our service like knowing we are doing it at His bidding. The passion I have to serve Pastor Johnny should not even compare to the passion I have to serve Jesus!

I believe laziness is a sure sign that we are apathetic to our calling. Each born-again Christian is gifted by God and called by God to exercise that giftedness. Each one of us is to be committed to exercising our spiritual gift within the context of the body of Christ. This is not optional.

> But the manifestation of the Spirit is given to each one for the profit of all. (1 Cor. 12:7)

The church must go to work. Jesus said to each of the seven churches of Asia Minor, "I know your works" (Rev. 2:2, 9, 13, 19; 3:1, 8, 15). Jesus expects His people to be active in His work. A lazy Sunday School will be devoid of God's blessings. We need to understand that blessings are the result of blisters! Leaders cannot sit idly by and watch people become lethargic toward the great work of reaching people, teaching people, and ministering to people. Paul warned young Timothy, "Do not neglect the gift that is in you" (1 Tim. 4:14). Paul was "keeping his sacred trust" by reminding Timothy of his duty to "keep his own sacred trust."

> **We need to understand that blessings are the result of blisters!**

4. Is there an absence of courage?

Does the church today need to get a spiritual backbone? Do we need a good dose of courage?

It takes courage to get the job done, so courage is on every leader's job description. It took courage for Joshua and Caleb to exhort the people to move into the promised land in spite of the opposition of the other ten spies and their report of the giants in the land. It took courage for Shadrach, Meshach, and Abednego not to worship King Nebuchadnezzar's image. It took courage for Daniel to continue to pray even though he would be thrown into the lions' den for his action. It took courage for Queen Esther to approach the throne of King Ahasuerus without his permission. It took courage for young David to take five stones and his slingshot against the champion

Goliath. It took courage for Jeremiah to prophetically pronounce the captivity of Israel to the Babylonians when others were calling him a traitor to the country. It took courage for John the Baptist to rebuke Herod for his adultery in taking his brother's wife for his own.

> The LORD is my light and my salvation—whom should I fear? The LORD is the stronghold of my life—of whom should I be afraid?" (Ps. 27:1 HCSB)

Courage is an inward battle. Circumstances and situations may prompt the need for courage, but ultimately courage is a man's struggle with himself. He must decide if he will do what he knows he should or whether he will take the road of least resistance. Author Larry Bielat said, "Taking the path of least resistance is what makes men and rivers crooked." Courage is forging ahead with what is right in spite of your fears. In fact, courage is not even needed if there is an absence of fear. Leaders who confront an inward fear take a giant leap forward in their growth.

Courage spreads like wildfire. When followers see their leader exert great courage then they are emboldened. Billy Graham once said: "Courage is contagious. When a brave man takes a stand, the spines of others are often stiffened." This is precisely what happened when brave David killed Goliath.

> Therefore David ran and stood over the Philistine, took his sword and drew it out of its sheath and killed him, and cut off his head with it. And when the Philistines saw that their champion was dead, they fled. Now the men of Israel and Judah arose and shouted, and pursued the Philistines as far as the entrance of the valley and to the gates of Ekron. And the wounded of the Philistines fell along the road to Shaaraim, even as far as Gath, and Ekron." (1 Sam. 17:51–52)

People follow courage, not titles. Position gives you opportunities, but courage gives you influence. It is difficult to follow a title, but courage has a draw all of its own. It is no wonder Paul established many churches and developed many spiritual leaders. Everywhere he went he was being opposed, yet he courageously presented the gospel and did not waver on the truth.

It Depends on Whose Hand Its In
(Written by Paul Ciniraj/Adapted)

> You place a basketball in my hand and we can play a pickup game of basketball. You place a basketball in Michael Jordan's hand and you get six NBA championship rings. It just depends on whose hand it's in!
>
> You place a football in my hand and I can toss it to my grandson. You place a football in Peyton Manning's hand and you get a $19 million dollar contract. It just depends on whose hand it's in!
>
> You place a mathematical formula in my hand and you get confusion. You place a mathematical formula in Albert Einstein's hand and you get the laws of relativity. It just depends on whose hand it's in!
>
> You place a rod in my hand and I can beat an angry dog away from me. You place a rod in Moses' hand and he will part the Red Sea. It just depends on whose hand it's in!
>
> You place a stone and slingshot in my hand and you get a kid's toy. But you place a stone and slingshot in David's hand and you slay the giant. It just depends on whose hand it's in!
>
> You place two fish and five loaves of bread in my hand and you get a couple of fish sandwiches. But you place them in Jesus' hand and 5,000 men are fed. It just depends on whose hand it's in!

> You place some nails in my hand and you might get a birdhouse. But you place some nails in Jesus' hands and you get the forgiveness of sins. It just depends on whose hand it's in! (Used by permission.)

Paul said the glorious gospel was committed to his sacred trust. He then exhorted young Timothy to keep that which was committed to his sacred trust. I believe he would say to me, "Oh Allan, keep that which is committed to your sacred trust!" And may I conclude by saying, "Oh dear Sunday School leader, keep that which is committed to your trust!"

THE PASSION OF SUNDAY SCHOOL IN HD

---

passion: a powerful emotion or appetite (*Webster's II New College Dictionary*)

CHAPTER 12

Eat Up with It

We live in a day of spiritual passivism, a day of spiritual tolerance, and a day of spiritual mediocrity. We desire to offend no one by our doctrine, our convictions, and our teaching. This mentality has naturally spread to our living. It is now rare to find a sold-out, on-fire, hot-hearted child of God. In our attempt to be palatable to all, we have become distasteful to God.

This has even spread to the clergy. Many ministers have lost the fervor they had after accepting God's call into the gospel ministry of Jesus Christ. Our calling has now been relegated to a vocation with which we seek good salaries, benefits, and places of service that will enhance our ministerial appeal and add clout to our resume. The fire that was once found in our bones has become smoldering ashes. A deal with the church has replaced the zeal of the Lord.

Apathy is so prevalent in the church today. Someone said that Americans are apathetic, but then again, who cares. We need to recapture that moment of awe when God's grace called us out of darkness and into His wonderful light! Like Jacob, we need to return to Bethel, the place God encountered us and called us. Once again we need to feel the emotions of both honor and humility when God said, "You are my chosen child."

In my childhood years, my three brothers and I were always playing ball. My mom used to say, "You boys, eat, sleep, and breathe ball. You boys are eat up with it." Well, I think it is time we Sunday School leaders were "eat up with it." We need to be eat up with the Word of God; we need to be eat up with the gospel; and we need to be eat up with loving and serving others. It is time to bury apathy and live passionately as we serve in the ministry of Sunday School. May we be consumed with the ministry that God has called us to do. Would not anything less be an offense? May our prayer be, "Lord, be ruthless in revealing areas of apathy in me!"

Perhaps the greatest reason we still look at Sunday School in standard definition versus high definition is a lack of passion. We have lost the zeal that once drove us to excel. Church has become ho-hum because she is filled with lukewarmness. Passion is a force that drives us to excel; mediocrity is to the church what cancer is to the body as it brings about a slow, painful death. We used to hear people of days gone by refer to an on-fire believer who loved and served his church as a "churchman." It seems the church is running low on churchmen these days. I want us to see three men who loved the house of God and had a passion for her ministry.

Jesus and Passion

I believe that Jesus is the most passionate man that ever walked on earth. He was passionate about people, so He shepherded them.

> But when He saw the multitudes, He was moved with compassion for them, because they were weary and scattered, like sheep having no shepherd. (Matt. 9:36)

He was passionate about sick people, so He loved and healed them.

> And when Jesus went out He saw a great multitude; and He was moved with compassion for them, and healed their sick. (Matt. 14:14)

He was passionate about His relationship with the Father, so He did whatever He saw His Father doing.

> Then Jesus said to them, "When you lift up the Son of Man, then you will know that I am He, and that I do nothing of Myself; but as My Father taught Me, I speak these things. And He who sent Me is with Me. The Father has not left Me alone, for I always do those things that please Him." (John 8:28–29)

He was passionate about the truth.

> Pilate therefore said to Him, "Are you a king then?" Jesus answered, "You say rightly that I am a king. For this cause I was born, and for this cause I have come into the world, that I should bear witness to the truth. Everyone who is of the truth hears My voice." (John 18:37)

He was passionate about saving people, so He hung on a cruel cross.

> "For the Son of Man has come to seek and to save that which was lost." (Luke 19:10)

He was passionate about doing God's will above everything else.

> "Therefore do not worry, saying, 'What shall we eat?' or 'What shall we drink?' or 'What shall we wear?' . . . But seek first the kingdom of God, and His righteousness, and all these things shall be added to you." (Matt. 6:31, 33)

He was passionate about the house of God.

> Now the Passover of the Jews was at hand, and Jesus went up to Jerusalem. And He found in the temple those who sold oxen and sheep and doves, and the money changers doing business. When He had made a whip of cords, He drove them all out of the temple, with the sheep and the oxen, and poured out the changers' money and overturned the tables. And He said to those who sold doves, "Take these things away! Do not make My Father's house a house of merchandise!" Then His disciples remembered that is was written, "Zeal for Your house *has eaten Me up*." (John 2:13–17, *emphasis mine*)

I love John 2:17 and the language of it so much that I titled this chapter after it. Jesus had zeal and passion for the house of God. His passion was so consuming that John repeated the psalmist who had previously described it by stating He was "eaten up" with it. John did not say He had a passion for His golf game, His lake house, His favorite sports team, or His bank account. Now there is not anything wrong with these things in their proper place. The issue is what place do they have in our lives? We should have a passion for the house of God as Jesus did. It was a sacred place dedicated to the things of God. He never ran businessmen away from other places, but the house of God was different, and He held it in high regard. He had respect for the sacredness of it and the purpose of it. It was not to be regarded as any other building.

> **We should have a passion for the house of God as Jesus did.**

Christians today have passion; the question is, where does that passion lie? Do we have a passion for the house of God as Jesus did? Can we say that the zeal of His house has "eaten us up"? Sunday

School leaders should be consumed with the ministry to which God has called us. If we had on-fire, passionate Sunday School leaders, then it would solve 90 percent of our problems. We would not sit around wondering if Sunday School still worked because we would be too busy working it. We would be completely consumed in reaching people, teaching people, and ministering to people. Sunday School is the church's greatest venue for involvement. It can be argued that Sunday School is the gauge by which a church can measure her zeal for the house of God.

Sunday School is the gauge by which a church can measure her zeal for the house of God.

I am grateful Jesus was passionate about the kingdom of God. This I know, if He were not passionate about it, then neither would we be passionate. Remember, if you want to know the temperature of a movement, then stick the thermometer in the leader's mouth. Passion communicates. Passion tells everyone that you really believe this. Passion also sells. It tells everyone that this is worth believing; this is worth the commitment of your life. A lack of passion also communicates. It notifies everyone that this is not that important and that you can take it or leave it.

Haggai and Passion

The people of Haggai's day had been given permission by King Cyrus of Persia to return from captivity and rebuild the temple (Ezra 1:1–4). We know from Ezra and Nehemiah that much opposition existed to this project, which made the work most difficult. So the remnant that returned for this very express purpose said it was not time to build the Lord's house (Hag. 1:2). Yet God said He would take pleasure in the rebuilding of the temple and would be glorified in it (Hag. 1:8). Haggai, by revelation from God, responded to the people.

> Then the word of the Lord came by Haggai the prophet, saying, "Is it time for you yourselves to dwell in your paneled houses, and this temple to lie in ruins?" (Hag. 1:3–4)

God wanted His temple rebuilt, and Haggai was passionate about delivering God's message to His people. "Paneled houses" were considered the type dwellings that kings lived in (1 Kings 7:3; Jer. 22:14). The people had time to build their nice houses but did not have time to build God's house. The difficulty of opposition prevented them from building God's house but not their own house. It is always easy and convenient to find a reason not to do God's will. There is always an available "good excuse." Benjamin Franklin once said, "I never knew a man who was good at making excuses who was good at anything else." The people returned for the express purpose of rebuilding the temple, but they got quickly sidetracked by opposition and their desire to build their own houses.

On five occasions Haggai asked the people to "consider."

> Now therefore thus says the Lord of hosts: "*Consider* your ways." . . . Thus says the Lord of hosts: "*Consider* your ways." . . . "And now, carefully *consider* from this day forward: from before stone was laid upon stone in the temple of the Lord." . . . "*Consider* now from this day forward, from the twenty-fourth day of the ninth month, from the day that the foundation of the Lord's temple was laid—*consider* it." (Hag. 1:5, 7; 2:15, 18, *emphasis mine*)

The word *consider* means "give careful thought to." God was asking them to examine themselves closely and carefully, and we should do the same. It really is true that your checkbook and calendar expose your priorities. Time and money are two of our most valuable resources, so where we spend them speaks volumes as to what we value. You see, time management is really not time management; it is priority management! Money management is really not money management; it is priority management! Simply put, you allocate these two precious commodities on your priorities.

The Jews seemed to forget why God had called them out of exile, so He raised up the prophet Haggai to remind them to place their priorities in the house of God and not their own houses. It seems Haggai knew Matthew 6:33 before it was spoken by Jesus. God is a reasonable God so He asked them to "consider." He tells them that He will be pleased if they rebuild the temple and will be glorified by it.

> "Go up to the mountains and bring wood and build the temple, that I may take pleasure in it and be glorified," says the LORD." (Hag. 1:8)

God also let the Israelites know that He would not bless their disobedience.

> "You looked for much, but indeed it came to little; and when you brought it home, I blew it away. Why?" says the LORD of hosts. "Because of My house that is in ruins, while every one of you runs to his own house." (Hag. 1:9)

God has obligated Himself to bless nothing but obedience. Misplaced priorities cannot draw the blessings of God. He is not pleased when the ministry of the church lies waste and in ruins while we live in our "paneled houses." Things have not changed from Haggai's day. We are still so consumed with our own personal agendas that we cannot see God's agenda. Perhaps there is no sin that the church is as guilty of today as the sin of preoccupation. We are so "eaten up" with our plans that we have forgotten God's plan. Our materialistic society tells us to get more and keep up with the Joneses. We have come to believe that possessions equal happiness, so we slave away after that which will not last. We have many committed Christians, but as a general rule the things of God have taken a backseat.

In Haggai's day the issue was building the physical house of God. Today our greatest issue is building the spiritual house of God, and Sunday School can do it! We need the passion of Haggai in being focused on God's agenda. We need Sunday School teachers who are "eaten up" with their class, their lessons, and reaching out. We need Sunday School leaders who are "eaten up" with enlisting people correctly, training leaders, and starting new classes. We have got to take our Sunday School ministry seriously and work at it tenaciously. We have got to eat, sleep, and breathe Sunday School! If you will not work the Sunday School ministry, then who will? If you will not be passionate about reaching people, teaching people, and ministering to people, then who will?

We have got to eat, sleep, and breathe Sunday School!

Paul and Passion

The apostle Paul gives us another great example of a man "eaten up with it." He ate, slept, and breathed ministry. He was always overwhelmed with Jesus. He was always busy apprehending that for which he was apprehended (Phil. 3:12). He consumed himself with the concerns of the church. He toiled day and night to spread the gospel. He was a man on mission and would not turn one iota to the left or the right. Oh, to God that we had more Christians like Paul who would exhaust themselves in the eternal cause of the call of God on their lives, who will count the cost and be counted on, who will press on while being pressed on, who will fight the good fight while being fought against!

If you are a Sunday School leader, then lead with everything in your being. If you are a Sunday School teacher, then teach with all your might. If you are an outreach leader, then reach out with a great zeal. If you are a care group leader, then minister wholeheartedly. If you make coffee for your Sunday School class, then make the best coffee in town. Whatever you do for Christ's sake, give it your absolute best and nothing less!

> Whatever you hand finds to do, do it with your might; for there is no work or device or knowledge or wisdom in the grave, where you are going. (Eccles. 9:10)

When I think of the apostle Paul, one word quickly comes to mind, *consumed*. Paul was a churchman obsessed with the ministry God had given him. He lived to permeate the world with the gospel and to establish churches in every town. He was consumed with his mission as evidenced by the hardships he endured.

> "Are they ministers of Christ?—I speak as a fool—I am more: in labors more abundant, in stripes above measure, in prisons more frequently, in deaths often. From the Jews five times I received forty stripes minus one. Three times I was beaten with rods: once I was stoned; three times I was shipwrecked; a night and a day I have been in the deep; in journeys often, in perils of waters, in perils of robbers, in perils of my own countrymen, in perils of the Gentiles, in perils in the city, in perils in the wilderness, in perils in the sea, in perils among false brethren; in weariness and toil, in sleeplessness often, in hunger and thirst, in fastings often, in cold and nakedness." (2 Cor. 11:23–27)

Paul was a man that would not be stopped. He laid everything on the table for the Lord and held nothing in reserve. He was not going to back up for anything; nor was he going to back down from anything. The words *retreat*, *compromise*, *give in*, or *give up* were not in his vocabulary. He would not tuck tail and hide; neither would he hightail it and run. He was a man focused on his God-given goal and was motivated to accomplish all that God had entrusted to him as an apostle laying the foundation for the Gentile church.

> Besides the other things, what comes upon me daily: my deep concern for all the churches. (2 Cor. 11:28)

Whatever motivates you, describes you! Paul loved the church and was motivated to establish and strengthen churches. Paul's deep-seated passion for the church is seen in the extremes to which he went to help them. We see his motivation in action with the church at Corinth.

Whatever motivates you, describes you!

> Now for the third time I am ready to come to you. And I will not be burdensome to you; for I do not seek yours, but you. For the children ought not to lay up for the parents, but the parents for the children. And I will very gladly spend and be spent for your souls; though the more abundantly I love you, the less I am loved. (2 Cor. 12:14–15)

"Now for the third time."

Passion will make you want to minister *continually.* Passion will keep you on the job. You may occasionally wish to stop, but you cannot. Sunday School leaders often have to carry their spiritual jumper cables around and reenergize others. Like Paul, a passionate person does not need a jump start; they are the ones jump-starting others. Passion gives you that something *extra*. It moves you beyond the ordinary and makes you *extra*ordinary. Oh, how we need Sunday School leaders who will move beyond the ordinary.

"I am ready to come to you."

Passion will make you want to minister *expediently*. Passion will get you moving. Zealous people are movers and shakers because they so believe in what they are doing that they must do something about it. They do not have to be begged or coerced; they stand ready, and when opportunity cracks the door open, they dive in.

"And I will not be burdensome to you."

Passion will make you want to minister *effectively*. Passion will not allow you to do anything but your best. Passion brings out the best in us and will not settle for anything less. Mediocrity dies where passion exists! The most effective Sunday School workers are passionate people who are there to help ease burdens, not be a burden. They are givers, not takers.

"For I do not seek yours, but you."

Passion will make you want to minister *worthily*. Passion will take the high road. Passion lifts you to a new level because you want your zeal to be caught by others. Therefore, you will do nothing to harm your cause in the minds of people. Passionate Sunday School workers understand that the cause is greater than any one individual.

"For the children ought not to lay up for the parents, but the parents for the children."

Passion will make you want to minister *unselfishly*. Passion will cause you to lose yourself and find others. Passionate Sunday School workers know that they are there to serve the ministry and not vice versa. They are not looking to see what they can get out of their service; rather, they desire to put into the ministry and make it better.

"And I will *very gladly* spend."

Passion will make you want to minister *gladly*. Your passion will become your greatest joy. Paul did not run from church to church with a frown on his face. He enjoyed his work, and he enjoyed people. Likewise, a Sunday School leader should not be a sourpuss with a grim, negative outlook on the ministry. Nehemiah and Ezra proclaimed a great principle to the people of their day: "For the joy of the LORD is your strength." (Neh. 8:10)

"And I will very gladly spend and be spent for your souls."

Passion will make you want to minister *tirelessly*. Passion will cause you to expend yourself, even to the point of losing sleep or missing some meals. You will live for it, work for it, cry for it, and die for it because it gives you purpose for existing. Sacrifice is a natural by-product of passion. John 3:16 informs us that God so loved us and was passionate about saving us that He *gave*. Passionate leaders give to the point of emptying themselves for others.

We will never develop a high-definition Sunday School if we do not have passionate leaders. Sunday School leaders should learn all they can about how to enlist and train workers, how to grow a class, how to implement Sunday School at multiple hours, how to lead a leadership meeting, etc.; but if leaders are not characterized by a great zeal for the ministry, they will greatly hamper their efforts. The people at First Baptist Church Woodstock kid with me by saying that when I visit lost and unchurched people I do not ask them if they have asked Jesus into their hearts; I ask them if they have asked Sunday School into their hearts. We all get a good laugh out of this, but deep down I take it as a compliment because it lets me know that they have caught my passion for Sunday School. Would Martin Luther have ever brought about the Reformation if he were not passionate about his theology? Would Martin Luther King have ever led effective change in civil rights if he were not passionate? Was it not

> **Great causes require great passion, and Sunday School is a great cause!**

passion that caused Jeremiah to prophesy against his own people when he entertained not doing so (Jer. 20:9)? Would the apostle Paul have ever traveled the world under difficult circumstances to preach the gospel if he were not passionate? Great causes require great passion, and Sunday School is a great cause! So, come on, leader, get eaten up with it!